LOVE and a Map to the UNALTERED SOUL

through
Tina Louise
Spalding

Other Books by
Tina Louise Spalding

Great Minds Speak to You

Making Love to God

Jesus: My Autobiography

LOVE and a Map to the UNALTERED SOUL

through Tina Louise Spalding

3⦾LIGHT
Technology
PUBLISHING

For information about special discounts for bulk purchases, please contact Light Technology Publishing Special Sales at 1-800-450-0985 or publishing@LightTechnology.net.

Illustrations by Leighah Allen

ISBN: 978-1-62233-047-8

PO Box 3540
Flagstaff, AZ 86003
1-800-450-0985
1-928-526-1345
www.LightTechnology.com

Dedication

This book is for all the people on this planet who are confused about love or who believe in love but don't know how to access it. It is for people who are closed but who wish to open. It is for people who are lonely and want communion with others. It is for all those beings who want peace instead of war. It is for all of us.

Contents

CHAPTER 29

Preface

LAST NIGHT I HAD A VISION. IN IT, A LIQUID METAL HEART APPEARED in my mind's eye, and two streams of children, one on either side of the heart, ran toward me. Then I felt a huge surge of expansion as my heart chakra burst, overflowing with the sensation of love. I gasped, overwhelmed by its power. Another wave of love surged in my chest, and my arms flung wide in an ecstatic expression of openness. I began to channel Christ consciousness. I spoke words that seem vague now but were so clear at the time, and they gave me my next assignment, this assignment: to write about love by channeling beings from a higher frequency — Ananda, Jesus, and Mary Magdalene — who all have something to say about our desire for love, how to define it, and how to find it.

Ananda, my guides and teachers, have asked me to write this preface to give you an idea of the growth and personal development I've had to accept as I bring these books through. The vision described above is an example of some of the experiences I have as I journey through this expanding consciousness. I am often given visions or channel information, both verbally and in my mind, at the strangest times, such as in planes and coffee shops.

Let me backtrack to when the book *Jesus: My Autobiography* (Light Technology Publishing, 2014) was being written so that you can get a glimpse into the life of an ordinary person who has been given an exceptional spiritual assignment. I channeled that manuscript in forty consecutive sessions over about a two-month period. I was alone, and I did not know what would transpire on its completion. Jesus came through as the last contributor to my second book, *Great Minds Speak to You* (Light Technology Publishing, 2013), a compendium of twenty deceased and iconic people, and the morning after that final chapter was completed, he asked me to write his autobiography.

"You've got to be kidding!" I thought. I am going to be perfectly honest here: My first thought was that this was dangerous, very dangerous, and it might even get me killed! For some reason, images of the pope and swarming black helicopters filled my head.

I was shocked as these thoughts tumbled through my consciousness, but somewhere deep in my mind were these ideas that the church would not tolerate what it would consider blasphemy, and it would put a stop to this revolutionary act. Where were these ideas coming from? I was not religious or fearful (at least in any conscious way) of any church that I knew of, yet here were anxieties I had never experienced before. Fortunately, I am a student of human consciousness and a bit of a historian, and I made an educated guess that these fears were taught to our culture for centuries through intimidating indoctrination and even under threat of death. Somehow, I too picked them up.

I did as I was told, and for thirty or forty minutes each morning, I began to channel a most fascinating tale of conception, growth, and enlightenment. The story of Jesus's life was intriguing, and my process was simple yet mind blowing. I was in for the biggest growth and spiritual evolution of my life! You see, channeling Jesus opens up everything for questioning: the foundation of our culture, my sanity, what's safe to say, and in the end, what is real. How do we decide what's real? That is the journey I have been on since June 2013, questioning everything, hiding, revealing, and eventually coming to terms with having the coolest job on Earth, really — telling Jesus and Mary's story and revealing the truths people always wanted to know. Who was Jesus, and what did he really do in his short but spectacular life? Was he married? Did he have children?

I told no one about what I was doing — for a few months, anyway. I had a small public channeling event late in the summer of 2014 with just a handful of local attendees, but fears kept coming up, and I decided to work on the book over the winter without exposing myself publicly anymore. I wasn't completely alone on this journey, however. My sons had been so moved by the teachings I was doing that they decided to jump on this unusual bandwagon and study with their eccentric mother, Ananda, and Jesus. That winter, we met for channeling sessions almost every evening around dinnertime, and my boys began studying the lessons of *A Course in Miracles* (Foundation for Inner Peace, 2007) in earnest. Our discussions were deep and fascinating, and I considered the fact that my young sons, only eighteen and twenty-two at that time, were on this path with me as a miracle in and of itself.

Hesitation to Heed the Call

Doing this "Jesus" work made me uncomfortable, though, and I began to procrastinate transcribing the book. Eventually, I put it aside and became caught up in my seemingly never-ending worries about earning a living. I channeled another manuscript through Ananda about Western society and its erroneous assumptions. It caused me fewer anxieties, and my mind could cope with it more easily.

I seemed stuck somehow, and I went back to an old way of making money — house painting. It was something I was good at, and the income stopped my financial fear in its tracks. I already had a part-time job that provided a basic income, so I added some house-painting contracts to the mix to generate more cash flow. The work was tiring, and I didn't spend much time on my real job: channeling Jesus and transcribing his words.

You might think that having two books published meant I'd "made it." Well, it's not that easy. There are 400,000 books on Amazon alone, and moving up that list takes time and effort. I could feel my limiting ideas dogging me, so I did what most of us do when we are confused: I kept doing what I'd always done but tried harder.

In July 2014, I was on an eighteen-foot ladder putting the finishing touches on a painting project when the ladder began to slip on the shiny hardwood floors. I slid down each rung of that ladder on my right foot, completely out of control and crying "No! No!" all the way down. I was in serious trouble, and when all was said and done, I lay on the floor, my Achilles tendon completely detached from my broken foot. I crawled to the phone and called my son Alex for help. Paramedics arrived and took me to the emergency room where I was told surgery was necessary if I wanted to walk again.

Channeling Jesus didn't protect me from my own frequency. My financial fears and limiting thoughts were of a low enough frequency that I attracted this experience into my life. What did I have to face now? I would not be able to work at all for three months, and I was never going up a ladder again. Reality hit me square between the eyes, and after surgery and a few days of acute care, I was at home sitting in a wheelchair with my leg in a cast. My guides, Ananda, were my companions, and Jesus's unfinished manuscript waited for my attention.

Yes, I took it as a sign. No more ladders! Writing and channeling were my purpose now. I didn't need to be told twice. So I dedicated the next few months to writing and polishing that most unusual project. I systematically worked through my anxieties, deciding that the unbelievable job I had been assigned, to tell Jesus's life story, was more important than any of my fears, and I focused on removing the money worries from my mind. As a student of these teachings, I realized I was experiencing one of the less evolved aspects of my mind, and I had to own it. After all, that was what Jesus was telling me. My life shows me my mind in all its loveliness and terror: a hodgepodge of mixed beliefs that make themselves known as my experience.

I was blessed with kind assistance from my sons and the companionship of another channel and good friend to get me through that time, but I have to admit most days were pretty lonely. The nature of the project I was working on and the endless encouragement and support of my nonphysical teachers kept me going, but I was financially broke and physically broken. You'd think I would have suffered deeply, but I didn't. The teachings helped me focus my mind on the good that was happening, and I slowly recovered and finished the book that I was told would change the world. Falling down the ladder had shown me the error of my ways and had gotten my attention to such a degree that all procrastination stopped and I became very focused and willing to do my real job, putting voice to Jesus's teachings.

That year, the universe orchestrated some wild circumstances that forced my hand. My life in 2015 was difficult, heartbreaking at times, and even overwhelming. It was no walk in the park by any means, but as a result, I gave up my part-time job and began a year of footloose living. I had no car, no predictable income, and no home to speak of. I was humbled in many ways, inspired in others, and always supported — sometimes by people and sometimes by faith.

After Facing Your Fears

Now I have thrown open my life to Spirit, and I let it lead me where it wants me to go. Every day, my guides show up in one form or another to write, teach, offer a Skype session to someone, or make a video, and it continues to be a miraculous journey into the unknown! I have started to travel a little and hope to share the work with many more people. Jesus and Ananda have told me this work will touch millions of people around the world. Who am I to doubt them?

I tell you this story because it's good to know the simple life and dedication creators put into their work. Writers or artists or channels or musicians — creative people know that life goes on, and if they are lucky, they get a great book or painting or song out of it all, but the truth is, when they are alone and working, they don't know. They don't know whether their art will even be seen in the end, but they listen to the guidance coming from within and pray they aren't crazy to follow the muse.

Now, this book has flowed out of my mind, through my voice connected to Spirit, and still my life looks quite ordinary (except that I channel Jesus and Mary). I write, exercise, and have a few close people in my life (not too many). Now I am out of the channeling closet! You all know what I do and whom I talk to every day, and it's okay. My fears are gone, and now I just work. I see how this process and these words written through me help people all around the planet. I get emails almost every day from well-wishers and people this work has touched. I have stopped doubting and being fearful, but it has taken a while. As you go through your journey with these teachings, you too will have questions and fears and doubts, but if you stick with it, miracles will happen.

I hope this book about love helps you as much as it has helped me. During its creation in 2015, it has shown me many of my limiting thoughts about love and when I close instead of open, when I need to forgive. It continues the great love story of Mary and Jesus but gives us the woman's side of the story. I am grateful to have the opportunity to hear Mary Magdalene speak so eloquently and so humanly.

Thank you for joining me on this journey. I read these books just as you do, as a student of love who is curious and searching for answers. I am no different from you. Something miraculous has happened, however: That veil that separates Spirit from humanity has parted for me, and it gives me great pleasure to share the tremendous fruits of that experience with all of you. Peace.

— Tina Louise Spalding, January 2016

Introduction

THIS IS A BOOK ABOUT LOVE, AND IT IS IMPORTANT. LOVE IS LACKING in your society and in your personal experience.

We are Ananda. We are teachers and guides, and we speak through this being as a gift to the world. That sounds arrogant, but it is not meant to be. We are grateful for the opportunity to bring this information forth. This channel who is using her body-mind complex to facilitate this communication is of great value not only to us but also to you because she is facilitating your evolution.

Love is the answer to all your problems, and there are many, many problems on your planet. You see problems of scarcity, sickness, war, fear, and broken relationships. You see many, many issues in front of you, but they are all iterations of the same problem, which is a lack of understanding of what love is, how to achieve it, and how to access it as a frequency.

Yes, love is a frequency. Many of you think love is a feeling. Well, the feeling is the result of the frequency; it is not the frequency itself. This is an important distinction. Love is a frequency, and it is a high frequency — not like fear or jealousy or hunger or suffering or pain. It is high on the frequency scale, and to reach it, you must climb a ladder of sorts, your own consciousness evolution.

Now, some of you can access love, or that feeling you believe is love, but for many of you, this is a conditional state and not what we consider true love. True love is never-ending. It does not refuse or inflict punishment, it does not withdraw or have temper tantrums, and it does not punish. Love always is, and it always emits the same high frequency of absolute, unconditional caring and offering, of growing and creation.

As you read this book, you will recognize that many things you call love are not. Some things you call love are actually control, possession, anger, and jealousy. The reason we bring this information through to you at this time is that unless you define love properly, you will fear it. You will fear it as the anger you have received from the voice of a loved one. You will fear it as something that will take away your freedom. You will fear it as something that will limit you in some way or cause you pain. By this very fear, you demonstrate that you lack understanding of love. As long as you misdefine love, as long as you bring it under your umbrella of jealousy and control and loss, you will fear it, and you will not understand how to achieve the frequency required to receive it.

We must instruct you here so that you do not go further into this book thinking you know what love is. We must give you a proper definition: Love is the truth, of course. We are immersed in love. We are here to help facilitate your education about love as we experience it.

We have no judgments of you. We do not judge you for being black or white, fat or thin, rich or poor, educated or uneducated, African or American or French or German. We do not care about these things. Love does not judge these things, so you can see that there is a quality to spiritual love that is missing in your experience and on your worldly plane. We must treat you as beginners, and you must allow yourselves to be beginners, or you will not learn the lessons.

If you think you are already capable of spiritual love, you will not read this book; you will think it is something you already know how to do. However, if you cannot look on every brother and sister on this planet and feel love or compassion for them or offer them your money, your food, your home, or your gentle, healing caress, then you do not love, and you do not know how to love.

This is the problem that faces your planet at this time. Yes, we see your world as a planet; we are extraterrestrial in that we are not of your world. Some beings among our group (for we are a group consciousness) have lived in physical bodies on your plane, so we understand the necessities of survival in this harsh world in which you find yourself, but many of us have lived on other planets in what you would consider other star systems, and we continue to do so. We are not what you call dead; we are what you call evolved. We have the ability to communicate with you across time and space and density in a way that is hard for you to comprehend. Some of us have never lived in the physical bodies that you call home. Some have always lived in the energetic realms. Those ones need explanations as to what it's like to live in a body, to be driven by a body, to be "cursed" by a body (it is not a curse).

Misconceptions about Love

We observe you from a higher place, a higher realm. We observe the planet Earth as beautiful and fertile, a precious jewel in the universe, and we see what you are doing to her and to each other, and we despair. We do not feel pain the way you do, but we look on this experience you are having and shake our heads and know we must do something to help you, for you are on the verge of self-annihilation, of individual self-destruction. Many of you eat poorly, think terribly, and act inappropriately, and it is because you do not understand the realm of love. You do not understand how to reach the realm of love.

You don't understand it because you have been incorrectly taught what love is. You learned about love from someone who hurt you, deprived you, or forced you, so you associate those pressures with that word. As you grew up, you might have associated love with something you'd rather avoid, such as being pressured to perform sexual favors or fending off inappropriate sexual advances. You linked those discomforts and feelings of oppression with love. That is not what love is either.

As you grew into adulthood and perhaps married or entered the work force, you may have made other associations with love: restriction, limitation, fear, and domination. None of these things is love. If you've entered your middle-age years, you might think that love does not last. You see that these things called marriages, these relationships, sour, and love sometimes turns to hate. But love never turns to hate. That is not its nature; it is always the same. Once again, you are bewildered and misinformed about what love is.

This is why this book is being written. You are immersed in a society that does not understand what love is, yet you think you do. This book explores this conditioning and some of the incorrect teachings about love. This is a disciplined and deep exploration of what it is. Because you have so many areas in which love can be but is not applied, you feel victimized, as if you have been abandoned by love. In fact, you have abandoned love simply because you do not know what it is.

This being or this essence that you call God is love. It is always available for you to dip your toes in, raise your minds into, and open your hearts to. There are many ways you can access this godly essence of being that which is love, but you are not taught how in your society. You are taught to watch television and drink alcohol and overeat and attack one another. These are the ways of your world. So we must bring to you the ways of our world, which are loving and kind and forgiving.

Many great teachers have come to your planet and brought these ideas. You know that, as a group, we work closely with the being you know as Jesus in bringing through truth, or true teachings, to Western society, and we have all been placed together to assist you in raising yourselves out of the old ways, out of the old religious doctrines of Christianity that are not assisting you at all. We come together now to bring you the new Christian doctrine, which is one of unconditional love and forgiveness.

This truth came to your planet so many years ago when Jesus walked on the soils of the part of the world you call the Middle East. Those soils are now decimated and crumbling. They are dry with war and fear and hatred. Those soils must be watered with the essence of love once again, yet they cannot be unless all of you in the Western world who are in charge of the collective expression of consciousness are taught how.

We begin with you. We begin with the individual you think you are, and we are going to educate you. So please come to this book knowing that you do not know how to love, that you are as a child stumbling through a thicket of underbrush and need help. You need a grown up to lift you in his or her loving arms, show you the landscape, brush the dirt and thorns from you, and soothe your wounds so that you may look far and wide and see that there is a beautiful land about you. You have simply become lost in the thorns and brambles of confusion.

We are here to assist in that process. We are here to lift you out of your fears and out of the overwhelming constraints of conditioned thinking.

We are here to open your hearts and minds and hands to receive that which is your true right, the light and love of God.

We are Ananda. We are here to bring this message to you. We want you to enjoy it. Yes, we know your language; we are part and parcel of it and have become very familiar with it. We are bringing through many teachings, so do not despair; we are here, helping you along your way to awakening and helping you along your way to a heart-opening appreciation of what love truly is.

— Ananda, October 9, 2015

PART 1

Expand Your Definition of Love
Ananda

CHAPTER 1

The Unaltered Soul
Seeks Experience

THE BIRTH PROCESS YOU EXPERIENCE IN YOUR PHYSICAL REALM IS a demonstration of love, but not in the way you think it is. You think that two beings who come together in love produce a child, but as you know from your worldly experience, this is not always so.

We are speaking about a much higher spiritual principle here. We are speaking about the desire for life. So we are going to go into the subject of life because that is love. Consciousness that you experience in your physical plane is an aspect of love. This is not how you are used to seeing it. You think of it as an experience, as your life, but really consciousness is experiencing, and this consciousness has always been. We call it an unaltered soul, that consciousness that desires life and experience and that is presence and love. We are redefining love here for you, dear ones, but do not panic. Do not think that we speak a different language. We are merely telling the story as it is, not as it has been told to you, because the story you have been told is causing many of the problems on your Earth plane at this time.

Consciousness exists. It is a loving thing, an expressive thing, an all-extending and forgiving energy that pervades every part of this universe. Some you see, and some you do not. Yes, there are many aspects of this experience that you do not see or are not aware of, but there is this loving force that permeates everything. You call it God, but we do not like to use that word, as it has been contaminated in your society. We will call it Benevolent Force, All That Is, or the Divine Mind of Love. These are some of the names you can use for this force. This force is ever expressive, so it expresses itself through life. As it desires a particular kind of experience, it brings into manifestation a physical form through which it can gather that loving information. It will, in fact, create a physical structure that you know as a body-mind complex to experience specific things.

From your point of view, you look at an effect and think it is a cause. You think that the body of the child causes consciousness to arise. That is not so. It is consciousness that causes the body-mind structure to arise, so it is very different from what you have been taught. This is what we call aspects of love manifesting — because life is love and love loves life. This is exactly what is going on here.

Consciousness chooses to experience more of itself and come to a deeper understanding of everything. It chooses particular physical forms to have particular experiences. For example, in your society, a male form is going to have a different experience than a female form. A male form in your society exerts different influences than a female form exerts. So there is a choice made by consciousness to manufacture — yes, manufacture — a form that would be considered a body-mind complex of a human individual into which loving consciousness is inserted. This is the beginning of the loving experience of life — consciousness creating a physical form.

This consciousness that desires a physical form brings together two beings who are appropriate genetic material to produce the physical structure required. There is a lot of deciding and choosing before the sperm and egg come together in the mother's body. This is all decided in spirit, in the nonphysical. It is all arranged and prearranged by beings of higher consciousness in association with the consciousness to be inserted in the physical structure. It is not random. This is not a random act of sexual intercourse that spawns a random child. No, this is a concerted, focused effort of consciousness to bring forth into the physical realm a particular shape, form, and style of physical structure and a particular shape and style of experience.

This is a very loving act on the part of consciousness, a perpetuation of the eternal life that is known to be so. It is a perpetuation of opportunities for growth and expansion of consciousness. It is the opportunity to express consciousness itself through physical, material creation.

These are all aspects of divine love. These are all aspects of divine mind expressing itself, but you do not think of it this way. You think of life as random and opportunistic, but it is not; it is profoundly loving and organized, and it is planned beyond your ability to comprehend at this time in your experience.

Focused Consciousness

Material structures are brought together through this essence of loving, focused, creative expression of consciousness. The physical, material world is a result of love, of consciousness focusing itself into physicality for particular experiences. We want you to understand the sacredness of life. We want you to understand the sacredness and purpose of your life, and this will allow you to begin to love yourself. We want to bring forth into your understanding the profound comprehension that you are divine life manifested, that you are a divine spark of God mind manifested, not some random act of biology that allows you to hate yourself and see yourself as insignificant. You are a divine act of God love that is self-expressing. If you begin to see yourself in this way, as this divine spark of God mind, then you will be able to offer yourself the love and kindness and respect you deserve because you are indeed that.

You are all divine aspects of God mind, and when you see a little baby, we want you to think of it that way. We do not want you to think of it as a biological consciousness that is a blank slate with no understanding — far from it. That little being comes in with great passion, desire, and understanding, and it is profoundly connected to the God mind. It has clarity of purpose and thought and self-expression that you lose on your plane. So to those of you who are parents or impending parents, we want you to treat that little being who comes through you as what it is. It is not a baby; it is a divine aspect of God mind temporarily housed in a small physical structure that is in great need of nurturance, unconditional love, and kindness and has been put in your care for that purpose.

Now, not all of you were raised that way. Not all of you were raised in unconditionally loving homes or embraced by unconditionally loving arms, but we want you to know that you are loved unconditionally. God loves you unconditionally. This benevolent force that permeates everything created you to experience, so you have such an energy — an ability to tap into this part of yourself — but you undermine yourselves greatly when you focus on your individuality and physicality. These are mere side effects of physical experience. The true gem that you hold inside of you is your connection to the Divine, and it is given to you through your emotional guidance system — your feeling, emotional self. That is why little children who are so full of emotion, joy, and happiness cry the second their freedom is thwarted. They are pure emotion in that sense. They are connected to the Divine through their feeling selves, yet in your world, this process of conditioning is very powerful, limiting, and hurtful. Have compassion for yourselves because you have been put through this powerful and hurtful and limiting process in your society. You are lost from the truth of what you are.

You are love manifested. You are indeed a divine spark of God mind physically incarnated for a short time as you travel through this experience housed in a physical structure you call your body, which you mistake for who you are. It is not who you are. It is the car you drive during this period. You have had many cars before, and you will have others in the future, but this make and model gives you a particular experience, so you chose it.

We want you to know that the physical structure you have chosen, the one that you reside in now, has been chosen for a very good reason. It is going to bring you the exact experiences you need to learn and to expand your consciousness. We want you to love the life you have. In this moment, you are in the perfect place. There have been no mistakes or errors in your life. Every experience you have had has come from love to show you where you are out of alignment with love and to show you where you have been taught incorrectly and have believed incorrectly.

In this moment, we want you to forgive yourself for the past. We want you to forgive everybody for the crimes you think they have committed against you because, in this moment, you are exactly where you need to be. You have come to this book because of those experiences.

We want you to begin to love yourself now. We want you to look at your body and know it has not done anything that you have not asked it to do. It has no volition of its own, even though you have been taught that it does. It does only what the mind directs it to do. It eats only what the mind directs it to eat. It says only what the mind directs it to say. It acts in accord with the mind that directs it to act, so it too must be forgiven and loved now.

From this place forward, we want you to begin to love your life as a demonstration of divine mind, and from this place, we want you to begin to love your body as a demonstration of the opportunity to experience, for that is what the body provides. It provides you with an opportunity to experience viscerally that which you believe, and it gives you the opportunity to communicate, into and with other minds, those beliefs and ideas so that you can hear them, see them, taste them, and feel them. When you know that they do not taste or feel good or do not sound nice, you have a visceral feedback system that shows you where you are out of alignment with love so that you may return to love.

This journey you are on with us is a return to love, and this information will assist you in understanding how and why this experience has happened to you.

CHAPTER 2

Move beyond the Physical

THE IDEA OF LOVE IN YOUR WORLD IS A ROMANTIC FANTASY, SO THESE beginning chapters might bewilder you because you might not understand what we are speaking about. You have been taught that love is between a man and a woman, between a parent and child, and so on. These are simplistic and very narrow definitions of love, and this is where the problem lies. Because you do not squeeze the juice out of your life, you do not appreciate the many aspects of divinity that you experience. Bear with us a little while, dear ones, so that we might unfold this story for you appropriately, and yes, we will get to the romantic love relationship you are so curious about. These chapters are the foundation for understanding where the issues lie and the problems began, so we ask you to very, very earnestly listen to these words we are bringing forth.

You believe babies are new beings. They are new physically, but they are not new spiritually or emotionally or mentally. Many newborn babies have strong conscious contacts with what you call the nonphysical. They are in communion with their beloved teachers and gurus for a considerable time after birth, but before we go into that, let's consider their gestation. This is a very important part of the love story, as you will come to see.

As a consciousness, through passion for life, decides to be born into a particular time and place, it brings its potential parents together. They begin to feel the desire for a child or to make love to each other. Now, in your society, you are taught that your feelings are just that — *your* feelings — but they are how Spirit speaks to you and how your unborn children speak to you.

Your babies communicate with you in spirit, telling you that they need a physical body to experience personal consciousness evolution. So as a potential parent, you will feel this desire rise in you. It is the voice of your future baby whispering in your ear, "Please, please, make me, make me." Those of you who feel you would like to have children now can see it as a profound act of love, these unmanifested spirits speaking to you through your feelings.

As these beings come together and create new life, there is, of course, great love present there. However, in your society, many of you are so defensive and angry and fearful that often these sexual encounters are not really lovemaking sessions. They can be quick and "dirty" rendezvous at parties or even actions instigated in anger. We do not want you to ever have sex with somebody you do not have feelings for.

It is important to understand that the frequency you bring to that act will affect the frequency of the being who might come into your life experience. If you are in a hateful relationship with somebody and continue to have sex with that person — perhaps facilitated by drugs or alcohol because love is not there and you must disguise your feelings or your reticence with inebriation — you are going to invite into your life a being of like frequency, and that being will bring with it the troubles of that frequency. So you will perpetuate this dysfunction as you perpetuate the energy in the act of coming together. This is something we want you to think about if you engage in sexual activity with people you do not like or love.

If you are "not yourself" when you participate in this act of communion, if you are drunk or high on drugs or in a fearful or agitated and negative state, you might bring through a child who is of that frequency. High frequency beings — intelligent, spiritual, creative beings who have a high life purpose — will not come into those frequencies. But beings who are desperate to come back into physicality, such as addicts or beings of low ambition, will find that acceptable and will align with that frequency. It is very important for you to understand this. Now, this sounds judgmental; it is not. It is simply what is. It is all frequency. Everything is frequency aligning with itself, but enough of that story.

Love Drives Growth

Let's return to the being who has brought its parents together, and they have made sweet, delicious love together and have begun the process of life (from your point of view). Of course, life is never-ending. There is no such thing as death as you know it. It is merely a physical structure coming to the end of its usage. It's nothing more, nothing less. But in this process now, you have the physical structure that is going to house consciousness.

Now, this process of physicality's growth is driven by Spirit, not by the physical as you have been taught. It is driven by the energies of love and by the energies of creativity from the Divine. Yes, you are coming into a separated, physical experience, which is less than that of the unified, love-based, nonphysical experience, but it is still coming from love. Why? Because you need this experience. Why? Because consciousness must learn and grow and expand itself, and experience is a delicious way of doing it. It is the way consciousness integrates understanding into its greater self.

In physical experience, there is a visceral, very focused, three-dimensional, sensory experience that goes beyond the physical into the emotional, mental and spiritual, and it is this intense blend that downloads the information. This is why you cannot just learn from a book; that way is intellectual only. It is not visceral or emotional; it is only mental, and that is only one small aspect of what you are. Again, this is an issue we deal with later because you are far too mental and not emotional enough in your society.

The developing baby is just a physical structure. Consciousness does not enter at the moment of conception, as some of you believe. Consciousness comes in and out of that body hundreds and hundreds of times during the gestation period. It comes in to check out the frequency of the parents and to check out the frequency of the body. It comes in and out, in and out, to see how this experience will go. Sometimes consciousness will decide that no, this is not the right time or the right place, and another consciousness might take over the opportunity for physicality. This is generally the case. Sometimes a consciousness will not take over this space, and the baby will be miscarried, and this can also be a lesson for the parents. Sometimes great learning is to be had in such an experience, but that is another story. We will not go into it here.

We are speaking of love, and of course, all this being who is coming into this physical structure has and wants to do is to live. It wants to live out its beliefs, its ideas, its thoughts, its passions, its dreams, its creativity, and its growth. This is all love, you know; this is all love. The desire to connect and to experience is love. Once again, you see that your definition of love is very narrow. Consciousness' desire to come into physicality is love itself demonstrated.

You Visit Home Frequently

Consciousness will come in and out of this physical body many times before birth, and at times, it will reside in that physical structure for a little while and then leave again. It will reside in that physical structure for days or weeks, and then it will leave again. It is testing the waters, you see. It does not want to set itself up for a situation that is not beneficial. It does not want to set itself up for a frequency that is out of alignment with it. It must bring itself into a place that is compatible. As the birth date approaches, consciousness begins to reside more fully in that physical structure, but even after birth, it leaves much of the time. That is why babies sleep so much: They are off in the nonphysical, learning and growing and discussing the experience. Yes, you discuss this birthing experience, this incarnational experience, with your guides and teachers every time you sleep.

Sleep is an important aspect of your conscious experience because you cannot tolerate being in the physical, separated in such a profound way, for very long because you are connected to Spirit. You are Spirit manifested into physical structure, and you must go Home frequently. You go Home every night, every time you nap, and that is what new babies do. They go Home because they miss Home. Home is love and forgiveness. It is all-embracing, loving energy. This journey into separation can be a very big challenge for the newly embodied consciousness, so it leaves frequently. Sometimes it goes Home permanently, and that is what you consider an early death, a childhood death. Sometimes consciousness cannot tolerate the separation inflicted on it in this world. Sometimes it makes the wrong decision and comes into an incompatible frequency, so it cannot stay.

Here we counsel those of you who have lost your children early in life that it had nothing to do with you. There was no responsibility there. The child, the consciousness that manifested as the child, had other plans, had other needs, had other wants. That child, that consciousness, might even manifest in a subsequent pregnancy, so the child who survives after the initial loss might be the very same consciousness. You might be grieving unnecessarily — in fact you *are* grieving unnecessarily because life is eternal, and you are not responsible for anyone's experience except your own. You cannot force a consciousness to stay in the separated state. Each consciousness decides whether to tolerate it or not. Some cannot, so you must forgive them for going Home. You must forgive them for leaving you, and you must forgive yourself. You did no harm; you did no wrong. It is merely the way of things.

Heed Your Guidance System

People bring a divine aspect of mind into this separated world, for they are going on a journey. It is like a parent who prepares a backpack for a child going on a hike by making sure he or she has sandwiches and juice and some first-aid supplies. Spirit does the same for you, except Spirit packs the things you need in your guidance system, in your feeling, emotional body. It gives you a connection to love that is permanent, unwavering, and consistent, and it is given to you in the form of feeling. When you are born, you have a direct contact to love that is always with you, and it is always impeccable and accurate. You are not taught this, so you do not understand feeling. You do not understand what it is, but it is the umbilical cord that Spirit has given you so that you know how to get Home.

You come down to a world of separation, a world of misunderstanding and misteaching, but Spirit loves you so much — consciousness loves you so much — that when you get lost in that world (for you will get lost in that world a little bit, and some of you will get lost a lot), all you need to do is listen to this feeling place. If it feels good, joyful, peaceful, happy, or content, then you are on the right track to your journey Home. If you feel sad, angry, or lost, then you have become disconnected from love. There is something you have done, thought, or said that is unloving. Remember, words and deeds come from thought and belief; they cannot manifest from any other place.

So this guidance system is given to you, and it is your demonstration of Spirit's love for you, but you misunderstand it. You think feelings are bad. You think these intense emotions that go through you are negative, but they are not. They are gifts that you must come to understand when you go on this journey to love. The return to love is what you are here to do, and this part of it is very important. This feeling part of it is given to you as a divine reminder of your Home.

It is important for you to listen to this guidance system. Its attunement with love is impeccable, so when you are unloving, you will feel bad; when you judge another, you will feel bad. When you are hateful to yourself, you will feel bad, and it is not because you are being punished or because you are bad. It is because you have stepped off the path of love. It is because you have become unloving in some way. It matters not whether you are unloving to yourself or to another or even to an idea: When you are unloving, you will feel bad because your guidance system is telling you that you are not unloving! Your guidance system always tells you that you are made of love, from love, for love, and if you are not fulfilling that purpose, you will feel uncomfortable, sad, angry, or frightened.

You, dear ones, are love. You are made of love, from love, for love, and your guidance system is always, always in alignment with love. You already have that which you seek. It is inside of you. Look there.

CHAPTER 3

You Are Part of a Greater Oneness

WHEN A CHILD IS BORN INTO YOUR WORLD, MANY THINGS HAPPEN, SO let's explore this process a little bit. Once again, it is a physical manifestation of love — not in the limited way that you believe it is, but in the profound spiritual way of true creativity. This consciousness that decides to be born comes into separation for many reasons. Now let's look into separation philosophy.

As the physical structure comes out of its mother's body, you have a physical demonstration of what is happening in the psychological, spiritual form in some sense. Get comfortable here, and prepare yourself for a little spiritual theory. It might seem to be off topic, but it is not. You will understand its implications as we move forward.

From our point of view, we are not separate; we are a collective consciousness. We have said this many times throughout our teaching relationship with humans. We are Ananda, a group consciousness, and that means many beings have come together to bring forth this information and the collective experience that we have had. This collective is love based. It is all-forgiving, it is all-loving, and it is nonjudgmental. It is observant, however, and sees and reacts to what is. In your lower-frequency state, you are caught in what is called the karmic cycle. Now, we do not want to bring in words that you have no definitions for already, so we will just refer to it as that, but what we want you to know is that these apparent lifetimes you have — these apparently separated bodies and experiences that you call reincarnation — are all happening at the same time. They are aspects of a collective consciousness that we call the oversoul. The oversoul is, in some ways, very much like us: It is a collective of many incarnations. So what you think of as individual incarnations that take place in different slivers of space and time are actually not taking place in your space and time.

From your limited-consciousness point of view (and we are not being insulting here; we are merely saying it is limited and ours is less limited), in your bodies, which require you to focus very pointedly in one moment, you are unable to detect these parallel and synchronous lifetimes easily or very well. Why? Because it would interfere with your experience. It is hard enough for you to focus on one moment without having many other lifetimes inundating your consciousness. This is done for a purpose: You can focus on this particular experience, on this particular integration of experience, for that is what you are doing.

For example, when you read about swimming, you are told that this body dives into water hands first with the rest of the body following and is immersed in a liquid that might be either cool or warm. These are just concepts in the mind. You can read as many books about swimming as you wish, but you will not know how to swim or have any idea of how it feels until you do it. The experience of it will not be a true one but an imagined one.

This is what happens in your incarnational history, let us say. You have the opportunity to feel everything that you experience. You will feel regret, and you will feel enthusiasm. You will experience terror and joy and love and hate and fear and creativity and all of these different things. You experience them in this pointed moment of focus you call the now. And this experience, this visceral, temporal understanding, will be downloaded into what you consider the greater mind, or the oversoul, which is part of a greater and greater and greater Oneness.

A Life Is Planned with Great Care

You try to understand something from the pointed, one-moment now, and it is very difficult to understand from that pointed, one-moment now. Even we, in our collective, have greater consciousness that is more and more difficult for us to understand, so it goes on and on and on. Do not feel that you are handicapped in any way. You are not handicapped; you are focused on a particular purpose.

As a baby is born into this physical, separated structure, it is only one small aspect of what the oversoul is capable of experiencing and understanding, and that little being comes in with a particular destiny, let us say. Now, there is a great discussion on your plane about free will and destiny. Well, we are going to explain it a little bit. It will still not be adequate for the truth of the experience because it is incomprehensible in some ways, but we will bring words to it to the best of our ability.

It is as if you have the design for a house. You understand that there are structural designs for a house. There are heating systems and foundations and load-bearing walls and rafters and roofs, all of which are different aspects of the building process that must be planned out with experienced architects and engineers. If you are in a tricky location, you must have a very well-engineered house that is designed properly; and if you have the ability, the experience, and the abundance, you might hire a very good architect to design a beautiful house for you. If you are not so accomplished and abundant in your frequency, then you will have to cobble together something that will do. Lives are somewhat similar. There is no value judgment on these, however, as there is with the beautiful house or the shanty. From Spirit's point of view, each experience is valid and offers much education and elucidation of truth.

So this structure that is going to be your life is engineered in the very same way. The baby that comes through into what you consider a new life is not at all what it appears to be from your limited point of view and your limited education at this point. We seek to rectify that a little bit. This being has a life coming to it that has had much thought and much highly evolved consciousness put into it.

Let's go back to this idea of the blueprint. The foundation is the family you are born into and the current understanding of reality that your frequency allows you to have. This is the foundation that holds up the construction you call your life. Then you have the walls. Now, some walls, as you know if you have ever renovated a home, can be knocked down. They are somewhat movable even though they appear to be as solid as the other walls because they are not load bearing. Some load-bearing walls run down the center of your house and are required. These are similar to some of the principles that apply in your life. There are some load-bearing walls in the blueprint of your life, and these are events that must be experienced.

For example, you might choose to have children. You might choose to have a partner and give birth to two children, let us say. These might be structural elements of your life in this particular incarnation that are required for your experience and your education. These are considered load-bearing walls. If you interfere in a relationship and destroy it by being unloving, the powers that be will bring forth another experience of another relationship that will facilitate the manifestation of this particular experience. So it seems, in the life that we are speaking about, as if that person is destined to marry and have children, and that is so. That would be considered a non-negotiable point in that life.

However, there are other aspects of a building. Let us say you have some decks and some balconies and some other aspects of the design that are not considered mandatory but optional. These represent the choices you have. Of course, then you have your roof, which would be the understanding this life brings to the consciousness that experiences it. All in all, there are many other aspects of the design that can be freely chosen, such as the carpets, the wallpaper, the drapes, and these sorts of things. These are all up to you. They are your design, but the structure of the house itself is going to be somewhat consistent based on the blueprint.

The blueprint is decided by the incarnating consciousness with the help of the teachers and guides of much higher frequency who assist that aspect of consciousness to evolve and to experience. Because you are destined to carry on from the frequency of previous or alternative incarnations, you might be stuck with some things you would prefer not to be stuck with.

If you repeatedly become lost in the desires of the physical, material world and step away from Spirit, you lower your frequency over time. We know that time is not real, and you know that time is not real in some ways, but you believe in it, so we use those words to help you understand. But if, in your previous incarnation, you began to wake up and see that love is the way, forgiveness is the path, and compassion is a creative device of the Divine, then your frequency rises, and you will have different options available to you in your future incarnation.

These are some of the aspects that are decided on with these beings of higher consciousness. These are not just angels or guardians; they are often group consciousnesses, such as ours, who collaborate with the individual preparing to come down into this lower-frequency realm. We want you to understand that at this particular time, the Earth plane is vibrating at quite a low frequency. There are many beings in higher realms who admire you very much for having the willingness to go to this lower-frequency realm because of its intensely separate nature. It is very challenging to maintain equilibrium and equanimity in this environment. We applaud you for coming to this considerably higher-frequency representation of consciousness now, respective of your place and time.

So much consideration precedes what you consider a simple, physical birth. From the points of view of us, Spirit, and the consciousness contained with that little baby's body-mind complex, planning a life is far from simple! It is a miracle, a loving act. Why? Because this is the way you facilitate your evolution. It is a loving act to come into separation and to experience these aspects of mind you have not yet mastered but are floundering with a little bit. This is considered a loving act.

Understand the Life You Live

When you teach a child to walk, he or she sometimes falls over and is hurt, so you brush the child off and sit him or her on your lap and provide comfort and maybe a bandage for any wounds. You soothe the toddler with some comforting activity, and then you put him or her down again and continue to allow the child to explore walking. That is very much what we do between incarnations with our dear human friends and travelers on this cocreative journey. Spirit will comfort you and soothe you and mop your teary face and clean you up a little bit, but inevitably it is time for you to be plopped back down on the Earth plane, and you will learn to walk. You will fall, and you will enjoy yourself. You will play with bricks, and you will gradually become stronger and wiser, and eventually you will walk by yourself — and so on and so on.

You see the similarity with a baby learning to walk. Then, of course, the child wants to learn to run and is hurt again, and once again, parental energies come in and pick the child up, clean grazed knees, soothe the hurt, provide some nutritious food and hot chocolate and love, and once again set the youngster on his or her way. Through the incarnation process, you are soothed, coddled, nursed, and loved between lifetimes, and once again you are set on your way to grow and learn and expand yourself. There is great joy in that for the consciousness going through the process. A little child who is hurt will snuggle up on a parent's lap and have a little nap after he or she has been given some nutrition and love, but once he or she calms down, the child wriggles off that lap and heads out for more adventures. You are exactly the same. You cannot be contained. You are, by nature, growth-focused, experience-focused, expanding beings, and you love the growth, the expansion, and yes, the return home for the sweet cuddles and the loving nurturance of the unconditional heart of Spirit.

Understand the life you are living. It is a challenge at times, and we know you are deeply separated in your society, which is why we bring this material through: You can begin to understand what is wrong with your society, why you suffer so, and how to remediate those particular problems. They are solvable, dear ones. They are solvable.

CHAPTER 4

You Can Raise Your Frequency

SO THIS LITTLE BEING WE DESCRIBED HAS COME INTO THE WORLD, AND the consciousness experiences a great shock when it first enters what you call physical reality, this lifetime. In separation, there is great fear and confusion about the choices that have been made.

Imagine this baby in utero — warm, secure, completely cared for, and without a thought. It does not need to ask for food; nourishment comes naturally into its body from its connection to its mother. We want you to know that this is a physical demonstration of exactly what happens to your consciousness. Remember, the physical world is a reflection of your consciousness: your birth from this place of unity and absolute connection and peace down through what is at times a very painful journey for the individual and then out into what is again, at times, a very threatening environment. This physical reality you experience shows you exactly what has happened to your consciousness. It has been wrenched from unity and peace and absolute support and love, Oneness, into complete separation, and immediately you can see that a difficult journey begins and is either magnified or mitigated by the circumstances into which that being is born.

So if you come into a lifetime of abundance and connection and love because of your frequency, you will be nurtured and cared for. You will be wrapped up after a nice warm bath in a soft and warm towel and placed in the arms of a loving person. You will be fed and cleaned and looked after. This is what you would consider a high-frequency environment. Even though you are in separation, it is still a high-frequency environment, one in which your needs and wants are addressed. That journey into separation is less traumatic than the experience a being of a low frequency, who has made lots of negative or unloving choices through many lifetimes and has lowered the frequency of this current incarnation through that free will choice, will have. That person very likely will be born into something other than comfort. He or she might be born into poverty, into a place that is unclean or unhealthy, or even into arms that are unloving to reflect the fact that the consciousness was unloving in a previous incarnation.

Remember, karma is just a reflection of frequency. That is all it is. There is no value judgment in it, no punishment. Remember too that you all have free will. In any moment, you have the ability to be nice or not, kind or not, and loving or not. You make those choices. Your consciousness makes those choices. Nobody else does it for you.

Now, this is very difficult to look at from an objective point of view without feeling as if there is some very bad, punishing God at work, but we remind you that this is just frequency, choice made on choice made on choice. It does not mean you are unloved by that which you would call God. Remember that you have separated yourself from God to come into this incarnation, and that choice was seemingly made long ago. However, in the timeless, formless place of Oneness, that choice was made in the eternal now, and here you are, coming into this frequency as a reflection of past decisions that you made.

Assist Others

You look at innocent children who are suffering, and you think a cruel God is involved. Well, these beings who come into new incarnations are not brand-new beings. They have had many opportunities to love or hate, to be kind or cruel, and to help or hinder throughout their histories, and they have made choices over and over again, just as every day you make choices. They have made choices and are born into a world that reflects those choices. Now, this does not mean those countries that are poor are evil in any way. It does not mean that at all. All it means is that birds of a feather flock together, and beings of a like frequency come together.

It also does not mean rich beings who have lots of material wealth are better than those who have less. They have accomplished certain physical manifestations based on frequencies associated with ideas of material wealth. They are not better in the eyes of Spirit; they merely have certain reflections because they have mastered certain things. Now, the certain things that a wealthy baby has mastered might be things such as comfort or climate-controlled conditions in which to live because these can be the most basic distresses for a little baby who comes into a world that it is too hot or too cold. These beings who have mastered certain aspects of the physical material world might not have mastered other aspects they are born into. They might not have mastered the ability to be compassionate or to share or to be generous even though they may have mastered other things. In this life, they have the opportunity to master those things. They might be given great wealth and the opportunity to master generosity. They might or might not take that opportunity, and that then will be reflected — yes, you guessed it correctly — in their next incarnation. They may very well be without abundance in their next incarnation to experience what it is like to experience the ungenerous.

Each coin has two sides, and each situation has positive and negative aspects. As difficult as it is for you to understand at this time, this all works out in the end. This all works out as education, as consciousness expansion, as forgiveness, and as love, and these opportunities for growth and change and education are loving opportunities. You do not think of things as loving in this way; however, a being who is ignorant of love might be put into a life that is ignorant of love to show that person that this is, in fact, a loving reflection so that he or she might see where he or she is lacking.

You do not look at love this way. You think love is only gentle or coddling, but that is not so. Sometimes love is a firm hand. Sometimes love is a focused opportunity for growth and to see a bigger picture. It is very much the same as when a small child wants candy and an adult says no because the adult knows that eating too much candy could cause the child's health to suffer. That child, in its immaturity and ignorance, might scream and cry and throw a temper tantrum, but the wiser being, the adult, would say, "I am sorry. No, you are still not having any candy." Well, Spirit is very much like that, and it will indeed give you a firm no when what you want does not serve your greater good or your greater spiritual health.

Children come into many disparate circumstances. They come into many kinds of families and experiences. All the experiences are specifically designed to give them the opportunities to choose differently and to expand out of the frequency they find themselves in. This can come in the form of what you consider as trials and tribulations.

If you have a low frequency and are given the opportunity to forgive, you can raise your frequency. How does that transpire? Well it might be through betrayal. Somebody might betray you, and you are given the opportunity to forgive him or her. You might accept it or not, but if you take it, your frequency will go up. If you do not accept it, you will be stuck where you are or move lower still, and another opportunity will be given to you. We have to shift your consciousness from the coddled and comfort-focused Western mind to a greater, more-expanded comprehension of the lessons and experiences that the nonphysical is willing to entertain on this journey.

We want you to understand that this is where acceptance and forgiveness come into your experience of observing this world. In your acceptance of other people's pathways, forces are at play that you do not have the consciousness to understand. In accepting this reality, you will be able to live in this world in peace. Many of you in the Western world lament the conditions of this planet — and justly so. You lament them repeatedly as you watch newscasts about war and suffering, but all the while, you live in comfort and do nothing about the agony you see. This is not a good use of your wealth, your creativity, or your mind. If you really care for those beings, you will use your opportunities, wealth, and education to assist in transforming the conditions of some of these beings.

Just because people come into a frequency based on past actions and decisions does not mean you cannot assist them. It also does not mean you should sit there, year after year, lamenting the state of the world in a passive and inactive way while you fill your body with too much food and too many other delicious entertainments.

We do not want to come across as judgmental, but this lamenting of suffering without really doing much about it is interesting. You have a lot more power at your command than you believe you do. You are, in fact, godlike creators, but you have not been taught about this. You have been taught the opposite. You come into this world, and you are taught the wrong things, so you begin to see cause as effect and effect as cause. This means you see the world as a victimizing energy that does things to you. You see yourself as a powerless victim of a cruel and vicious god who plays with you on this plane. That is not what is happening at all.

You are the creator through your choices of experiences, and you can come to a place of acceptance and understanding that energies were put into play before this lifetime for you. If you can come to this understanding, then you can respond to the world in a correct way — not only as a participant in it, but also as someone who can accept and forgive the family into which you were born (even though that family may not provide you with what you think you should have), knowing that they are a reflection of your choices and your frequency. Your family has, in fact, provided you with an accurate reflection of where you were when you chose to come into this physical experience. Another benefit of accepting the state of the world is that you do not waste your energy or creativity on lamenting something that is, in fact, based on justice and a spiritual law that is playing out perfectly.

We are saying many things here, but the most important thing is that each being who comes onto this plane has done so based on the frequency of its previous incarnations. Each being who comes onto this plane has been given opportunities to raise its frequency through the blueprint of its life and will be given those opportunities at various times and locations throughout life. You are gifted with opportunities to become bigger, to become better, and to become more, and you are given a guidance system that functions impeccably. You are born with this connection to the Divine, and we describe it in great detail, so stay tuned.

CHAPTER 5

Your Inner Guidance System

THE IMPECCABLE CONNECTION YOU HAVE WITH THE DIVINE IS CONTAINED within you. One of the great illusions of your society is the idea that God is separate from you and is ignoring you. The opposite is true, in fact; you ignore the Divine. The Divine speaks to you through your inner guidance system — your feelings and emotions. Let us start at the beginning.

Remember that you have many simultaneous incarnations. It is not a linear thing as you have been taught. It is not one lifetime after another with the same personality shifting in and out of different bodies. You have a unique quality that holds a central place in all the different personalities you encounter in your incarnational patchwork quilt, let us say. It is very much like that except it is multidimensional and through many timelines. It is not linear.

Before this particular incarnation and in concert with consciousnesses of higher frequency — you call them angels, guides, teachers, and these kinds of beings — you looked at what you wanted to experience. Now, as an element of a greater mind — a greater oversoul, let us say — you would seem to be separate, but you are not. There are experiences that would serve, and there are understandings that need to be explored, so these are some of the discussions that take place — not verbally, but energetically, psychologically, and empathically with the beings of higher understanding.

You see, you are a little separated from Oneness when you are in the incarnational cycle. Even between lifetimes, you are not given the complete understanding of everything. It would be too much for that level of consciousness. As you evolve through millennia, you have access to more and more and more.

Your Spiritual Assignments

Let's sample a lifetime, for there are lessons to learn. In this (not completely) expanded state of consciousness, you have discussions with your teachers and guides, your higher self, and other aspects of consciousness that know more, understand more, see more, feel more, and have integrated more into their own senses of what is best. You are given assignments much as a university student is given assignments.

A professor who understands more, who has educated him- or herself in all the subjects being discussed, might assign essays. It is not the essay, in and of itself, that is important, of course; it is the research and the exploration of the subject that bring forth the paper. The same thing happens in your experiences in your life. Perhaps you have a child, for example, as the experience, but the journey through that experience, not the physical child, is the end product. It's what you learn, explore, feel, fear, and come to understand. It is the experience of having a child that is the assignment. The paper, or the child, is an effect, but the real value is in the experience. This is one way your assignments are given to you. They look as if they are in physical form, but it is, in fact, the experience of coming to that physical form that brings what your spirit is looking for.

You are given other experiences. One example might be forgiveness. You have great opportunities to forgive several times in your life, and they are not what you think. When you are given an opportunity to forgive, it is a great gift that the other offers you because it is through forgiveness that you come to a deeper understanding of love. It is through forgiveness that you come to a greater understanding of the suffering of the human mind, and it is through forgiveness that you master the physical world. So what might seem like a betrayal or a physical injury coming from another is an opportunity for you to grow. Many things like this are assigned to you throughout your lifetime. These are general structures. They are the foundation, or the structural elements, of an incarnation, and you decide on them in combination with other beings who have your consciousness evolution as their purpose.

Within those structures, you have a lot of freedom. You can grow your hair long, you can have certain jobs, you can drive certain cars, and you can live in certain places, and all of these things are fun for you to add into the mix. Of course, you have free will. In every moment, you can choose love or not, so even though a certain aspect or element of fate is decided, there are other things that you can choose to do. There is truth to both the idea of destiny and free will; they both play out.

As you evolve, you will come to understand these subjects more and more. You must remember that we always use words you understand and concepts that are familiar to you to describe things that are very different from what you believe they are. As you evolve, as you step into higher and higher levels of consciousness, some of the relative discussions we bring forth will seem less than accurate, but that is because we must use the words you believe in and the concepts you understand in order to elaborate. We must use those things to teach you more and more, and eventually you will understand that some of the things you learned in kindergarten were not exactly correct. These are truths, paradoxes, and joys of expansion, so any shortfall, any story that we tell you that seems to cause a little consternation, may be because you understand greater principles or you have a feeling that there is something else at play, and you may very well be right.

We are keeping it simple here for those of you who come with curiosity and perhaps a limited understanding of some of these spiritual principles. We do not mean to be condescending in any way; we are merely trying to explain in a way that makes sense.

Be Gentle with Your Little Ones

The assignments given to you are programmed, let us say, within your inner guidance system. When you come into physical existence, you are a new physical structure that houses all experiences and your connection to the Divine in your feeling/emotional self. You have many memories, many attachments, and many desires that are predetermined. When children are born, they are very different from their siblings and parents, and you wonder how that came to be. Well, they chose their parents for certain reasons that might be genetic rather than personal or emotional or psychological. The parents might be genetically suitable for creating the physical body that the being needs for its experiences. A very large number of variables are at play. It is not as simple as you might think it is.

Every being comes in with a guidance system connected to those higher beings, to those higher levels of consciousness, that will provide continuous and uninterrupted instruction, especially in the dream state. That is one thing babies love to do. If you are fortunate and are a new parent with a baby who loves to sleep, know that it is not just wasting its life. The baby is growing and learning many, many things in the nonphysical as it closes its eyes.

As the small child grows, it encounters other people's ideas, thoughts, beliefs, and values, and this is, of course, where society begins to provide some problems for the newly incarnated being. Because you have stepped away from love for a very long time, your society has some very poor habits, and children, when they first come in to this environment, can experience harsh treatment. They can be told off, smacked, neglected, and otherwise abused.

This is a very painful thing not only for the child who experiences it but also for those of us in the nonphysical who witness it. It is very difficult for us to stand by, but we must because you have free will and are allowed to do whatever you chose. We come here, of course, as educators, as facilitators, as holders of the light, and we ask you to take these lessons to heart so that these unfortunate cultural patterns can be put to an end.

This is where many of you have experienced distress, discomfort, and limitation: You had parents who did not know how to love or raise children. But all of you come in with a divine guidance system. This is what we want you to take from this, especially those of you who have young children and are trying to teach them to fit into this society. We ask you to be very careful and to bring more and more love to the mix. Bring more and more compassion, forgiveness, and kindness to the process of raising children because they are your teachers. They are the ones who will be in charge of the new world that is coming your way. They are the ones who will be your saviors.

You do not want to indoctrinate your children into limitation and fear;

you want to encourage them to expand and be creative. You do not want to teach them to sit in an office chair when their purpose is to write the most beautiful songs the world has ever heard. You do not want to condition them into financial fear when they are the most magnificent creators and will bring abundance to this Earth that has never been seen before. Their guidance is their gift to the world, and if you override it the way yours has been overridden, you will lose one of the greatest resources that is being brought forth on this Earth plane at this time.

Be gentle with your little ones. Their desires, their passions, and their strengths are going to save you, and you must be humble in your parenting. You must look around to see what has not been accomplished by your society's teachings and by your own disciplined and limited encounters with education and cultural imperatives. You must be honest about this and learn some new things.

Become that parent you wish you'd had. Open your heart and mind, and learn these new potential realities. Do not indoctrinate the next generation. Do not override their guidance systems. This is where most of your suffering comes from — the distortion of truth and the separation from your innate knowing — and this is what you must, as an adult, come to understand: You are disconnected from your guidance system. One of the first steps on a truly spiritual path is to begin to listen to how you feel and to base decisions on that insight. Begin to do what you want because it feels right and is good for you. In doing things that are good for you, you will be good for the world.

Listening to your feelings is not selfish, evil, or the devil's handiwork. It is the opposite. God speaks to you through your feelings, through your emotions, which have been given to you as a divine right, yours to indulge as you see fit — without hurting others. The difficulty comes when you have built a life that is out of accord with your true self, and that is what we will speak about next. When you have been living out of alignment with your feelings, out of alignment with what you would really like to experience, how do you deal with that? How do you deal with those beings you care for, those beings who have come to depend on you? How do you deal with them when you want to change some things because you are now coming to understand that your guidance system is your divine connection to that which you call God?

Follow Your Feelings

The training you have gone through in your society is very intense and begins very early in life, so you must understand early in this realization process that there is no quick fix to shift your life into what you think it can be. All of you desire freedom, creativity, and self-expression, but many of you do not realize that those desires are your map to the love that is the life of you being yourself. That is really what love is.

Love is honoring the self and listening to the guidance from that which you call God, that which you call your connection to the Divine. You do not think of it that way, but this is the foundational element of the love problems you hold in your life. You are truly looking for love in all the wrong places. This phrase is the truth of your pain, and it is the truth of your suffering when it comes to the special love relationships in your life because you have, in your separation from love, become confused.

You must remember the principles on which your Earth plane is founded. These begin with your belief in separation, or individuality, and that has created your experience here. You are deceived by your own story, the ego's story. Remember, the ego is separation manifested. It is all the fears and ideas and beliefs you hold about love being dangerous, overwhelming, and destructive in some way. That is really the frequency of this place. As you look around and see the wars, destruction, starvation, overindulgence, selfishness, self-centeredness — all of these things — you can see that the frequency this place holds is not a loving one. You taste love in your families and your love relationships, but even then the ego usually wins. We have come to bring you the truth of creation, the truth about what is going on in your minds and on your Earth at this time. Otherwise, you cannot fix the problem.

Many of you believe that finding the right love partner is the solution to all your problems, and if you can't find him or her and have access to that person's body whenever you choose, then you are going to be in dire straits. That is what your society promotes, and fear accompanies these teachings. You think you'll appear strange somehow, that you'll be alone, that you must keep doing what you are doing to keep those around you near you as friends, family, or lovers. It does not matter. You feel you will lose if you don't follow those teachings.

The truth is, you must look at the fruits of this belief system in your world right now. Look at the shootings, the environmental devastation, the wars, and the terror that are being wielded in this system that is the ego's playground. You must be honest with yourself.

Healing Your World Begins in Your Mind

Many of you have created safe little environments in homes that are comfortable, with food in the fridge and televisions to watch, but we want you to know that this is separation manifested as well. Many of you have no community, no intimate people who truly know who you are. Some people might see your social face and might think you are the being who you present to the world — the doctor, the lawyer, the mother, the alcoholic, whatever your presentation is — but they do not know the true you because you do not express it. The true you is the foundation of love, the foundation of what we say is God's love for you. You have been given feelings, desires, interests, curiosities, and passions for a reason. They are not given to you as torments to interfere with your job, and they are not given to you as torments to interrupt your special relationships. They are given to you because they provide the path that will lead you to the life you truly desire, not the one that has been marketed to you on the television, such as going to tropical islands or visiting ski chalets in faraway places. These are all marketing devices to get you to go to work.

You have been indoctrinated into a marketing system that is pervasive and universal. Even third-world countries seek to attain the images that are on television screens. You tune into your favorite shows, and you run to the kitchen during commercials, or you record those shows to watch later and skip the ads. You think this prevents you from being indoctrinated further. You are mistaken.

Television shows indoctrinate marketing in their subject matter, scripts, costumes, and relationships. You are indoctrinated into this world's belief system of the ego mind. The ego's thought system is a complete thought system. You cannot dip in and out of it and feel happy; you cannot participate in it in a partial way. The thought system that we and the other participants in this teaching are bringing through is also a complete thought system, one that is focused on love and forgiveness as a device to return the mind to oneness, to its full and complete and holy state. If you dabble in the ego's thought system as you go through this, you will feel profound conflict. You will feel fear because you have very powerful beliefs in the mind, each one asking you to follow it, and we are asking you to do things that the ego does not want to do. Forgiveness is the most important, and it terrifies the ego because the ego's food is judgment.

Judgment keeps this world going, and you can see that in how people judge each other. In that judgment, you keep wars going, and wars fund the planet at this time. We are being quite radical here, but we are telling you the truth, which is you must dedicate yourself to love if you want to see a transformation in the world you are looking at.

In living your life, you must begin to choose love. You must begin to make that decision for love that your politicians and warmongers and arms dealers will not make on your behalf. They will not do it for you. They are a collective consequence of the minds of beings who are fearful and afraid, and they believe in attack. This is where your healing must begin. It must begin within your own mind. It must begin within your self-understanding.

At this stage, you have feelings, and you desire something other than what you have, which is the case for most Westerners. Do not panic; there is not something particularly wrong with you. Realize that the world you experience is going to change and by changing your beliefs and thoughts, you will change the feelings you have.

Many of you are very stressed. You have jobs that you believe you must go to, but you do not enjoy them. Or you have jobs that are okay, but they take too much of your time, so you do not have room for anything else and cannot imagine shifting your world. You cannot imagine making changes without losing your home or your income. These are the terrors that arise as you begin to entertain the idea of listening to your feelings and doing what you want to do. However, you can begin slowly, in this moment, by just watching how you feel. This is the most important thing.

The now moment is the only place you have the opportunity to change anything, no matter how rich or evolved you are. It is in this moment when you have the only opportunity that is ever given to you. You are as powerful in this moment as the most evolved or the wealthiest being on the planet. We want you to understand that. In this moment, you have exactly the same choices as anybody has, and those are to choose a loving thought, a kinder thought, or a more authentic thought, and then you will have the opportunity to realize thoughts in action. Action always begins with thought.

Everything you do now arises from your belief that it will bring you something, even if it is a temporary pleasure. It shows you that you believe a temporary pleasure is more important than a long-term accomplishment. This is a belief that you hold. Those of you who are eating or drinking things that are unhealthy or watching unhealthy shows are choosing a short-term pleasure over a long-term accomplishment. That shows you that you believe the short term is more important. Even in the smallest action, you act out a belief.

These are some of the intricacies of thought and word and deed that you will come to understand as you go through this journey into self-education and self-realization. There is no other journey to take, dear ones. The journey of the ego ends in war and death and sickness; it is inevitable. Century after century, there is no evidence that it will bring you anything other than these things. As your ego-centered society focuses more and more on that kind of thinking, you will see war and hatred and devastation escalate.

It is time to make these decisions, so we are here to support that transformation, that shift in consciousness. And yes, it does take some time, but following the ego's path for the next few years will not take you any closer to happiness or eternal youth or the peace of mind that this path provides. Now is the time. It is time for you to choose love, which is the best choice for you because it is the choice for listening to your feelings, your smallest instruction from the Divine. Your feelings — your inner guidance system — are instructions from the universe telling you which direction to take next.

CHAPTER 6

Seek Love Within

IN LOOKING FOR LOVE IN YOUR SOCIETY, YOU ARE DEALING WITH A frequency issue. You live in a consciousness that is separated from Oneness and believes in death, the body, and many low-frequency ideas, yet love is a high-frequency idea. In fact, it is the highest frequency idea possible, because that is the frequency of what you call God or what you call your Home.

You see, you have come from a place, and you are made from the essence of that place, which you call love. You have not been told this story very often. It is a new story in your mythology, so we ask you to bear with us. You may have come across it before in other books or publications or videos, but we ask you to listen once again.

The greater part of you — the true you, if you will — is still connected to the Divine. You seem to be separated because you seem to be in a body that lives in a violent and hateful world, a fear-based world where death exists. It is a very real-feeling illusion, just as the nightmares you have can feel so real that you think you will die. It is a dream such as those. It is generated within your consciousness, and that is the most difficult part of this journey for you to come to understand.

In some insane moment eons ago yet a moment ago, an aspect of Divine mind decided that it would experience individuality. It wanted to experience separation to try its own game, so to speak. In that amazing moment of creation — for it was a moment of creation, albeit a misguided one — your consciousness plummeted into separation, and the incredible contrast of the fear in that experience brought terror into the mind. In that moment, the separated consciousness completely abandoned its home, and it tried to create something that would placate the terrors and intense feeling of separation. That is what this world is: It is your mind covering up what you have chosen to do, which essentially is to abandon love. When you hear the tales of God being love and you look around this world, you know there is some terrible disparity here, some terrible disconnection, because you see a world that is not full of love. You see a world that is far from it. So this God in your mythology makes no sense. But in this story (which is the truth), you are the creator of this place! You are the one playing out your desires, your fears, and your guilt (let us say) for making that decision and separating yourself from Oneness.

In creating this split — for it is a split mind that you experience — you have hidden from yourself the great fears, great guilt, and these concepts, and you have put them out in the world on the movie screen that plays in front of you. You seem to be the innocent one and okay within yourself, but there are bad guys out there. Death lurks around each corner, and war rages, but you still think you are the innocent one.

Everyone feels as if he or she is the innocent one, the unfairly treated one, the one who has nothing to do with this objective world that is coming at him or her at full force. The truth is, you are only aware of half of your consciousness; the other half is projected outside you and seems to be the world that you are experiencing and that is happening to you. As you experience this, there is still a connection to Home, and it is in your feelings, your emotions, and your desire for love. Part of you is well aware that love is your home and unity is the place where you are going to be happy once again. But because the mind has an unconsciousness and a split nature — a projecting nature, a fearful nature, and a guilty nature — it looks for love out in the world, and that is not where it is.

You Are Always Guided by Love

Here we get to what we call the special relationship. We have indulged ourselves in leading up to this subject because it is important you understand some of the fundamental principles of creation. It is important you understand where you have come from and what is going on here; otherwise, you cannot find the love you seek.

You are, in fact, guided by love all the time, but you do not know it. It is in your feelings. In your feelings, there is what we call an invisible umbilical cord to the truth that is your higher self, which is still connected and resting in the arms of that which we call God, or unity consciousness, and that connection is what we must return you to.

Now, in your misinterpretation of feelings, you feel a lack of love, a separated consciousness, and fear. So in your society, you have been indoctrinated to seek out a special partner, the one who will solve all these problems for you, but of course, this is a delusional state, and you are mistaken. You are also a victim of your own judgment and ideology, let us say. You believe the world is objective and the other beings who populate your dream are real and truly separate. In that illusion, you are able to maintain a semblance of peace, a cease-fire. You can see in your relationships and in your experiences that as these things come closer to you, you begin to feel fear. You begin to feel judgment, and you begin to feel all the beliefs, the guilt, the anxiety, and the anger that you have hidden in the world. You begin to feel them as they approach, and that is why the ego is so determined to keep you separate: It must deal with its greatest fears if you allow people, places, and things to become important to you.

You can see this in the extreme example of the hermit who feels okay when he or she is alone or is never around people. You will also see it in the person who isolates him- or herself and feels somewhat okay in his or her apartment or house when he or she does not have contact with people. Yet when that person goes into the world, all kinds of feelings arise, and he or she believes someone else is causing that discomfort. These feelings are within you. They are not anywhere else but within your consciousness and because of the grand projection, you think you feel these things because of what others do. They are all within your own consciousness, within your own mind. You have been such a great creator, such a creative generator of images and thoughts and ideas, that in an effort to keep yourself tolerant of this grand separation, you have believed your own dream, and it has become a nightmare.

As you venture into love by your definition, you begin to feel the deep fears and anxieties of the egoic consciousness, whose natural state is separation. Remember, you have chosen to separate yourself from One-ness. You, in fact, have chosen to abandon that which you call God, to abandon love. In your belief system, you go against yourself when you seek love in another, and that is why the ego gets very upset when you seek love. It fears the connection and communion because, in essence, in choosing separation and coming into this world, you act against that which you said you believe in. Of course, as you approach love, things like separation cannot be tolerated, and individuality must be put aside for communion, compassion, and kindness.

This is the battle you all face, the battle of seeking love in the ego's world. You will not find it there because in the ego's world, separation, war, death, and sickness rule. These are all demonstrations of your sepa-ration from love, for love will not allow those things to thrive. Love will not allow the kind of world that you have to survive in. So in the ego's world, turning toward love means losing everything you have come to believe in: your body, your wealth, your home, your car. It believes that in choosing love, you will lose all those things, and this is one reason your relationships are so fragile, one reason you have a difficult time staying in love with anybody, because you are, in fact, in a level of consciousness that is counter to love.

We are here to teach you how to choose love, how to shift your con-sciousness from that which you call the world to that which you call heaven. You can have heaven on Earth, but you must know how hell is created. That is what you see playing out on the screen of your life at this time. You see minds indoctrinated in fear, separation, and judgment that are becoming more and more empowered. Rather than love, you choose attack; rather than peace, you choose war. We remind you once again that this is the collective mind playing out. As you sit your children in front of violent television shows or you watch murder movies or blockbuster shows in which the hero kills everybody who opposes him or is "bad," you do not realize you are feeding the war machine, falling into the trap of the egoic consciousness frequency.

These teachings are difficult to hear because they go against every-thing you have been told is true. They go against your society and the very thoughts you have in your mind, but you must understand that your thoughts are generated from your beliefs, and your beliefs are implanted in your mind. You come with a belief in separation and fear that is the nature of this place, and it is further indoctrinated through mass and social media.

The love you seek in another is in you. The love you seek in another must first be connected with through your divine connection to what you call God, or All That Is. We are not speaking about a religious connection; we are speaking about a nonjudgmental, accepting state of being that forgives everything it sees, that knows what it sees is being generated from a consciousness that is separated from love. Once you understand this is happening, you will be able to make different choices, have different thoughts, and empower different beliefs. But until you realize what has happened and is happening to you, you will seek love but not find it.

Free Your Mind

As we mentioned before, you are profoundly indoctrinated in the special love relationship, so some things we bring up will make you very uncomfortable. You have already undertaken a tremendous feat of learning. You visualize yourself as an ordinary human being walking through the world, perhaps with a family, a job, confusions, desires, frustrations — and passions, if you are lucky. But what you are is a profoundly conditioned and indoctrinated being. Your world of buildings, cars, forty-hour workweeks, cell phones, and televisions is completely unnatural. It has been building over the past decades. The industrialization and the urbanization of your world, of course, has been evolving for centuries, but the modifications of your minds have been taking place for the past several decades.

You have in your world what you call conspiracy theorists, and mainstream organizations consider them to be radicals, freaks, and paranoids. Yet they are onto something. There is a systematic program of indoctrination going on in your society. For some of you, this is difficult to process because you consider yourselves to be spiritual, and you seek truth. To acknowledge that there is a plan afoot in society to keep you in a low frequency is a distressing thought because you have been indoctrinated into believing it is a distressing thought.

The school system teaches blending in, and it shames and ostracizes students to get them to be compliant. This starts very early on because the system must mold young, pliable brains before they are seven years old.

Seven is a pivotal age in your psychological and spiritual development. There is an exceptional ability to learn in these early years, and it is a magical time. It is the time when Spirit speaks to you, when fairies and devas and otherworldly beings have access to the unformed, unindoctrinated, unaltered soul's mind. Societal constraints are inflicted on little children because that is what must be done to stop the natural flowering of the creative mind. So this is why school is mandatory and children are prepared for school with preschool and kindergarten; it is the way to control people.

Again, our teachings bring up uncomfortable feelings for many of you because when you actually begin to see what is happening to your children in your society, you might feel guilt about putting them in school and inflicting these constraints on them. You have been through the system yourself, and it is self-perpetuating. Once you have been indoctrinated for twelve, fifteen, or eighteen years — yes, even including your post-secondary systems — it is impossible to be free without reconditioning your mind.

We bring these ideas to you because the special relationship is one of the profound indoctrinations in your society. We do not need to belabor that point. You have heard the love songs and seen the romantic movies. You see, in modern society, the belief system of the ego is repeatedly indoctrinated in your mind. Everywhere you go, there are songs playing about love, romance, the perfect partner, and dying for your love, and all are the ego's stories.

In movies, you see stories of romantic love mixed with war. In the action movies purporting to be about the dominance of good over evil, the hero is always a man who is violent and aggressive, never kind or gentle. Death and violence are two main thrusts of the egoic consciousness, and they are linked to the special love relationship in these stories, so these cannot be separated in your reeducation program. They are part of the complete belief system of the egoic consciousness. Because of the romanticized and intense belief in the special love relationship, you might feel as if you are going to lose something as we present these teachings. You might feel as if you are going to lose the one thing that you believe could save you from the difficult journey you are on through the ego's world, and that is the special love relationship.

Women, in particular, are indoctrinated with this idea. They are indoctrinated to be passive even though they are educated and encouraged to go into the work force. They are also indoctrinated to worship the body and beauty. That means they are encouraged to behave within certain boundaries, such as working only when it does not inconvenience the pursuit of the special love relationship.

These are the two fundamental structures that hold up the ego's thought system, so we must approach this honestly with you. We must bring these thoughts and concepts and ideas into your conscious mind, and they will disturb you. Until you have done the lessons of *A Course in Miracles*, until you have immersed yourself and learned those principles that govern the Christ consciousness paradigm we bring forth, you will have a difficult time listening to these things because you will believe you are going to lose everything of value. That is not true. You will lose only those things that do not serve you. You will only lose things that are not generated form a place of love and are not in the best interests of your consciousness' evolution.

However, this means you will look different from those beings around you. You will begin to learn a new value system. You will learn the value system of Spirit, of Christ mind, and that is the reunification of the mind based on love. The path to that is forgiveness.

Be Patient with Yourself

As you read and come to understand these principles, we once again encourage you to read *A Course in Miracles*. Begin the lessons and feel the distress this new path brings up. The fact that it brings up distress should not surprise you. You have been profoundly courted and seduced into a belief system. It is not a few ideas; it is a complete system that depends on you to function.

Your entire society depends on the belief in the justification of war and violence and the pursuit of the special relationship to continue marketing the products and the wars that it creates, destroying the environment in the way it does, and keeping you consuming as it wants you to. These systems have been very long in the making. They are a sea in which you and your parents have been swimming, so you cannot clearly discern them because you have been immersed in them for such a long time.

Be patient with yourself. As you feel irritation arise, begin a journal to allow these thoughts to exit your mind and appear on paper. They will disturb you, and you will want to withdraw from this course of training, but when you write them down, you can look at them and go beneath the fear into the belief that creates the thought. Remember, your beliefs create thoughts, and your thoughts create feelings. These beliefs have been deeply implanted. Essentially, you have been brainwashed. These beliefs generate thoughts and feelings all the time.

When we introduce new ideas, you will have conflicting beliefs. When you want to learn these new things that agitate the mind, realize that your mind's natural state seeks peace, so it will want to get rid of the belief that is most recent and therefore least believable. Those of you who are on a path to awakening and seek self-realization must understand this process. The mind tries to get back to peace as quickly as it can, and to do that, it tries to eliminate the troublemaker, which is, essentially, our message.

To combat this natural state of clarification that the mind always seeks, you must write down the disturbing thoughts, go beneath the words and the fear, and ask yourself, "What is the belief that is generating this thought? Do I actually believe in it?" Unfortunately, some of you will continue to believe in it. Some of you will continue to believe that if only you could meet the right person, everything would be okay. Meeting the right person in the egoic consciousness is impossible, and that is the endless pursuit you are on, seeking the perfect person when there is no such thing other than you.

You are the perfect person, but you must be clarified and returned to your unaltered state. You must be returned to your true self, the unconditioned mind, and it is a process, dear ones. It is a process. To live your entire life seeking outside of yourself for that which you can never find is a delusional action, a never-ending process of suffering. We encourage you to hold firm in your desire for peace, to hold firm in your desire for a new world, and to hold firm in your desire for a truthful existence that is connected to Spirit, connected to the Divine, and expresses love and kindness in all its wonderful forms that are available to you.

CHAPTER 7

You Create Your Experiences

WE ARE BRINGING THIS IDEA OF DISRUPTIONS AND UPSETS THAT YOU feel in your emotional guidance system to the surface because most people's understanding of what is going on when they are upset is confused. When you are upset, you are off track. You are out of alignment. When you are upset, you are dealing with conflicts in the mind, and the mind cannot tolerate conflict. Let us go back into a basic understanding of the experience you have.

As we have mentioned, you have kept the parts of your mind that you can tolerate close by. You call this your ordinary consciousness and beliefs. You have put outside of you the things that frighten you and bring up conflict in the mind, those things that create such terror that you literally cannot live with them consciously. You place them in a very safe place where most people do not think to look for their demons or darkness. It is "outside" of you and in the movie you are immersed in of this life story you call the world.

Think about this "grand projection," as we call it. You have put outside of yourself the things that you have not reconciled — the things that you do not have a true understanding of — and that frighten you. And yes, you have put love among those things. You have put love there because in your separation from Oneness (in deciding to come into a separate body with an apparently individual mind and personality), you have chosen, literally, not love. The love we speak about is divine love, the love that God has for you and that you are made of. You chose other. You chose an individual experience, to come into a small self rather than the large self that you were generated within, so there is great guilt and fear hidden in the mind. You have put it outside of yourself, and that is why the world appears to be a frightening place and why you hide from it. That is why you keep yourselves in little homes and are fearful of relationships and of being hurt: You feel, as you get close to people, the unconscious guilt and fear that lives in the mind. You have not rid yourself of it; it is merely separated from your awareness. But when you get close to it, you begin to shake in your boots, so to speak.

Of course, you have your family, and you are close to them whether you want to be or not. That is, as we say, your first opportunity for love. It is also your first opportunity to see your fears because those are people you are close to from the time of your birth, and they have secrets and messages for you that you often misinterpret.

Now, we know you want to find the love of your life. It is the great dream of the Western mind to find that perfect person, and we will tell you how to get to that perfect place of love, but first we must explain what is going on in your mind, or you will not get there. Bear with us as we go through these technicalities and explain how to get to where you want to go, which is a place of peace and love and joy. Everyone on this planet wants to get to that place, yet you all look around and realize it is not there.

There is very little peace, even for those who live where no bombs go off. The mind you live in is far from peaceful. It is agitated, fearful, and often angry or ashamed or guilty, and these are feelings generated by separation. Remember, you were at one point unified with love — that is your Home — and you decided to come into separation. But the separation does not have to look as bad as it does on your planet; there are many societies in different galaxies and on different planets that are in the physical realm and are happier, more peaceful, and more loving. So we want you to know that separation, in and of itself, does not have to be hellish.

We are not telling you to wait until you return to Oneness to feel okay; that is what you are afraid of and what traditional religions tell you: You will only have heaven when you die. That is not so. It is often the case, however, that humans do not feel the experience of reunification until they die because they do not have the right information while they are alive. That is, of course, why we are speaking through this particular channel, so that you can have this information while living on the planet. It is more fun that way! We must delve into the hearts and minds of confused humans, hold their hands, and bring them out of the darkness so that they can see another way.

Your Experiences Reflect Your Frequency

Your first opportunity for love is in your family. Clearly, this is where your experience seems to begin. However, you are not a fresh pea out of the pod when you are born; you have many other incarnational experiences playing out in your higher consciousness. You are like the tentacle of a great octopus, and the body of the octopus represents your higher mind. You are but the tip of one tentacle, collecting information. Like the tip of a tentacle, you experience a particular time and place, and it takes time to experience. It takes time to understand things, and it is a demonstration of your great power and abilities to see yourself not as the tip of a tentacle but as a connection to all the other tentacles through the higher mind.

That is what is happening here with this being [the channel]. She is tapping into higher levels of consciousness. Instead of focusing out from the tip of that tentacle to the world around her as the source of everything, she has gone inward to the higher mind, and she is now experiencing both. That is where you reap the real rewards of the great consciousness you are. As long as you believe you are only that little tip, alone in your environment, you will be fearful and confused because there is a great deal of information coming down from the higher mind through that tentacle into your experience. If you ignore it or do not know that it is there, it will confuse you.

You have been taught that you are a little speck that is separate and alone, and you have believed that because you stepped away from Oneness. You refused Oneness. It was your choice. You were given free will so that you could create, but because of the conditioning in your society, you are using the information and the experience incorrectly. We must teach you how to use this experience properly, and to do that, we go back to your childhood.

You have memories, resentments, blame, and shame from your childhood. We must go there with you to help you understand what happened so that you can reclaim the parts of you that are stuck there. You came into this world with a certain set of factors you wanted to explore, and your family was one of those helpful elements. They were going to give you a particular experience to show you what was happening inside you. They are not separate from you. They are neither villains nor saviors, but they are reflections of the ideas in the mind that experiences itself as you.

For example, if you had a difficult childhood or you came into a family that was abusive in some way, you are not guilty of the abuse. We do not blame the victim. What we are saying is that when you came into this incarnation, the frequencies that you held, the experiences that you needed to understand yourself more fully, and the setup that you needed to live the life that you were destined to live played out in your family.

Some of you have come into this world with a very low frequency of self-loathing or self-hatred. A lack of love is what that is. It is not a sin; it is simply a lack of love, and you were born into a family that reflected it. They demonstrated, through experience, what you held to be true. Of course, you were wrong. How do you know you were wrong? It felt bad. When something feels bad, you know it's wrong. But when you look at it from a linear and materialistic point of view, you would say your parents were to blame for your difficult childhood if they were abusive or unkind. From Spirit's point of view, they were showing you your frequency and reflecting back to you something you were unconscious of, something you were hiding from, and something you needed to see.

So in this moment, when you look back on your abusive or unloving or difficult family, you can say, "Ah, they were showing me where I was, and they were showing me my lack of love!" Forgiving their behavior becomes possible because you can look at the situation correctly.

How will you know you are looking at the situation correctly? You will feel a sense of relief. You will feel a rising sense of peace, which is your guidance system saying, "Yes, you are on track! You are heading in the right direction, and this is the correct path." The path of forgiveness, knowledge, and self-understanding will always bring you a sense of peace. The path of judgment, attack, and hatred will always bring a sense of unease and discomfort, which is your guidance system saying, "No, you are wrong."

Revisit any resentment you hold for your parents or siblings. Reevaluate what that message was and whether it has continued throughout your life. In your Western world, you are taught that if a family member abused you and you continue to have those feelings throughout your life, the abuser is to blame because that person was the perpetrator and you were the victim. The truth is the opposite. By generating a negative experience, you are its creator. If those negative feelings of unworthiness or victimization have carried on through your life, then those feelings are coming from within, dear one; they are coming from within your own mind. Through the practice of forgiveness and by understanding the grand projection, you will first come to a place of tentative peace and then eventually profound peace. It will be through the practice of forgiveness and understanding that you generate your experience, even from the time of your birth.

Many of you blame the past for what you are now, but the blame is misplaced! The way that you are now is a choice, a decision made in this moment. "Am I going to be fearful, or am I going to be loving? Am I going to be judgmental, or am I going to be forgiving?" Your future and your creative power are held in this moment, and that is why it is so important to visit the past one more time to go through all those experiences that caused you pain and let them go! Realize that they arose from within your consciousness, and they were shown to you as a lesson in self-understanding.

If you are angered or upset by any of the words you have read here, you know you are wrong because you feel bad. Remember that your guidance system generates a feeling of relief when you are on track. So if we have upset you, then we now can become your forgiveness practice. Forgive us for bringing information to you that you do not like.

You will have many upsets as we share these teachings because you have been taught the wrong thing. Not only have you been *taught* the wrong thing decade after decade, but you have also *practiced* it decade after decade. It is deeply entrenched in your experiential world and in your learning mind. You have to unlearn some very difficult things, so if you are upset about some of the things in this chapter, we are happy to be your forgiveness practice. Forgiveness is something you need to practice, and we are very willing to help you with that.

Understand Your Conditioning

As you step into your new love life (your adult search for love) using the principles here, you will see that you have built many of your ideas, thoughts, and dreams on an unsound foundation, and this is why many relationships fail. You did not understand that this world is truly a figment of your imagination, and you did not have the ability to interpret your feelings correctly. Just as we have discussed your childhood, now we want you to really understand the conditioning processes that have been inflicted on you.

You have been taught from a very early age that the world is objective in that it has nothing to do with you, and it arises of its own accord. This teaching does not serve you because it is not the truth, and you know it is not the truth because it does not feel good.

When something outside you attacks you and you have no control over it, you feel as if you are powerless, and that does not feel good. When you are judged and then feel distressed because of it, you feel bad. It does not feel good to you, but because of your training — or we say *lack* of training — about your emotions, you misinterpret these actions from outside as just that: an objective reality that acts on you. That is not the case. You must begin to truly grasp the concept that you are the creator of all your experiences, that there is no vengeful God punishing you, and that there is no karma playing out in the sense that you understand it. Do not think that when you have been bad, bad things happen to you. No. You see a reflection, but it is not a reflection loaded with guilt or shame or blame; it is a frequency reflection. So in this understanding, you begin to feel a sense of relief because what you discover is that you are the captain of your ship. You are, dear ones; you are all the captains of your ships. You have come into separation to experience your Godlike creative powers along the lines that you choose, along the lines of your free will.

Many of the conditioned teachings in your society go against the idea that you have the right to live the life you want to live, and one reason those teachings have persisted is to keep you from finding your power and strength, which are your creative, Godlike abilities. For centuries the powers that be have not wanted you to know this information or to wield your free will — your free, creative mind — or to express yourself freely. They have not wanted this because it would infringe on their abilities to manipulate and control you.

This, again, is where the idea of conspiracy comes in, and it is real, dear ones! There has been an across-the-board manipulation of the minds of the general population, and it began in the early church. It began with the restriction of sexual energy, one of your most divine assets, and it has persisted by teaching you to be meek rather than the grand being you are. Some of those teachings you received from the church (we use the word "church" in general). Of course, the Roman Catholic Church wielded much power for centuries, but those teachings have dispersed into many denominations (some are a little more liberal than others), all of which pretty much tell the same stories that are, generally speaking, untrue. They have, however, taken snippets of the truth and sprinkled them in to give you a sense of hope, a sense that there's potential. What we are telling you now (and this might upset you a little bit) is that the very foundation of your society is based on the untruths that death is real, you are a sinner, and Eve was the perpetrator of the original sin. These are all lies that have been used to manipulate and control people.

Reevaluate the Importance of Money in Your Love Relationships

We provide this teaching to help free you from this prison that has been centuries — millennia, in fact — in the making, so you must keep it in perspective as you begin the journey. You must keep in perspective how much work it will take for you, as a victim of this indoctrination, to free your mind, your heart, and your creative self from these limiting beliefs and ideas. They are deep and broad in your society, and it is important for you to understand this at this stage of your development. You will dig at this for a while because it is a deep subject that has been long in the making and because the consequences of the indoctrination are pervasive and persistent. This is why those systems have worked so well: They have been uncompromising in their insistence that you follow them. The church was uncompromising in its insistence that you follow the rules. If you did not, you suffered ostracism, shame, or even death. Your school system is the same: It is uncompromising. You must follow a particular curriculum and attend classes at particular intervals. Otherwise, you will not be able to get a job.

Now, the system you play out your lives in is an artificial one. It seems normal to you, but from our point of view, it is an ego construction, and we do not support many of the concepts and ideas your society promotes. We are bringing through many ideas that will confound you a little bit, such as not working a forty-hour week for somebody else. Such concepts are challenged here because they are merely that: modern, ego-created concepts that serve a particular portion of your population and not the rest. Generally speaking, those who spend forty hours a week working for others are not happy.

The fundamental principles of your education system play into your special relationship concepts because of the idea of money. In your relationships, sex and money are big issues, so we must delve into them as they relate to the separated mind and to the special relationship. They are important in your disruptions and distorted ways of looking at the world. As we venture into this subject of love, you will dip your toes in many other topics because they directly relate to the idea of love and the special relationship.

As you enter your school system, your training continues to play out. Of course, your family, as a reflection of you, is where you begin your journey. Now looking back on it, you can see that perhaps there were some unfortunate beginnings, unfortunate seeds sown in those early years, but sown seeds do not necessarily grow. Sown seeds only grow when you water, nurture, and pay attention to them.

Now in your adulthood, you can do this self-analysis and see that you do not need to water and nurture and coddle those ideas. That is how they have stayed alive — through your attention to and care for them.

Focus on Memories That Bring You Joy

If you had unkind or abusive parents, it seems unfair to you, in the egoic consciousness in which you live, to let them off the hook, so to speak, but you are not letting anybody off the hook except yourself. You are stuck on the wall, unable to move, because of your obsession with the past wounds and injuries you believe were inflicted on you. You are imprisoned by that belief because you waste your precious creative force and focus on something that does not benefit you, on something that continues to play out in your life as long as you focus on it.

This is very important for you to understand. As long as you are deeply immersed in the unfortunate events of the past, you will bring that frequency into the present moment, which is the only place you can create, and you will attract to you things of that frequency. So when you forgive your unloving or abusive parents, you free up the present moment and can create a different future. When you resent, when you hate, and when you harbor these old wounds, you contaminate your present moment, and that prevents you from creating a new life, which is the ultimate self-abuse!

We know these ideas are challenging, but they relate directly to your love life because when you carry old resentments from your childhood or you hate your parents or other beings who participated in unkind activities in your early years, then you bring that frequency into the present moment and attract a partner of like frequency. If you were abused by your parents, guess what you are going to attract: You will attract an abusive person not because you are bad or stupid but because you continue to hold the frequency of abuse.

These are very important fundamental lessons in transforming your love life and in understanding the issue of frequency and magnetization. You magnetize your future in this moment, so you must direct your mind to things that make you feel good. You must focus your mind on things that make you happy. You must create, in this moment, the frequency you would like to experience. So if you concentrate on unpleasant memories (this can become an unconscious habit) or you repeatedly tell an old story about people who hurt you or the sins they committed, then you become the perpetrator. You do it to yourself because you bring that frequency into your creative present, and that is the only place where you have power to influence your life.

This act of forgiveness that we ask you to participate in is the most self-loving thing you can do. The beings who hurt you have moved on and are living their own existences, but until you forgive them, until you free up that part of your mind and reclaim that part of yourself, you are imprisoned in the past, and you waste your creative energy there. It will not stay there but will come into this present moment, contaminating your current frequency, and that is what we are concerned about. You can disrupt your current frequency in many, many ways, and this is one of them.

From now on, after you cut the ties to those memories, we want you to be very disciplined about how you use memory. We want you to focus on only nice things. Find experiences that make you smile, that bring you joy, and that bring you a feeling of peace and relief and excitement of some kind.

Memory is a powerful tool for the ego. It is one of its greatest collectors of crimes, we would say, so it is important to understand its misuse and proper use. Your memories should only be collected if they make you feel good, such as if they make you happy or inspire you to repeat something that previously brought you joy. Do not revisit the past to collect negative memories. You will contaminate the mind and feel an immediate feedback from your guidance system because you will begin to feel bad — and that is a clue that you are on the wrong track. Make sure that when you collect memories, you pay attention to how they make you feel. Even good memories can bring bad feelings.

For example, let us say you are single, and you had a great love. As you go back in your memory and lament the loss of that love, you do not feel good about it. If you go back and enjoy the memories of being with that person and use those memories as a testament to what you can re-create, you will feel better and will allow that memory to feed your frequency. It is not only the event but also how you look at it. Make sure that you always look at past events with a positive, loving, appreciative, and forgiving eye. This is forgiveness in practice. Judgment in practice is seeking evidence of crimes or sins and justifying hatred.

CHAPTER 8

How to Find Love

THE BODY IS ONE OF THE GREAT LIABILITIES YOU ARE FACED WITH IN this world. It is one of the major symbols of separation, so we reiterate the story of separation in which you "fell from grace," so to speak, and chose individuality instead of union or communion with oneness, with All That Is.

The body is made by the ego for its purposes. Your religious stories have taken this truth and contaminated it with versions of sin. The church promoted the idea that the flesh is sinful, that the devil uses the flesh, that it is unholy in some way. It is not completely untrue. The body is of the ego, and the ego is separation from love. The body encapsulates and symbolizes that which is not love. This is a challenging concept for those of you in the West because you have been laboring under the misconception that God created your body, and this is not so. God does not create temporary things. God is all-loving, all-encompassing, all-forgiving, and eternal in nature and structure, so things that decay over time, get sick, or die are not of God.

This is one of the greatest hurdles you must jump over as you learn nondualistic teachings. Remember, nondualistic teachings say that there is only one essence, and it is love. That is the only thing that is real. Anything else is an absence of love or an absence of the awareness of love's presence. In nondualistic teachings, the body is not real because it sickens and dies. It is mortal in that sense.

In dualistic teachings, which you have been raised on (remember, you have been deeply conditioned to believe these things), you believe in birth, in death, and in the body as a real thing! Now, as you sit there in your body, it is very difficult for you *not* to believe it is a real thing; you get lots of sensory input that tells you the body is real. You can see it, taste it, touch it, and hear it! This is interesting proof (as far as you are concerned) that the body is real, but you are using the body itself to prove it's realness and that is a self-fulfilling prophecy. You cannot, in fact, prove a body is real without using a body to prove that it exists!

This is a very difficult conundrum for the mind: You say that seeing the body makes it real, but the eyes are part of the body. We are not asking you to deny the body; we are asking you to focus on spirit. There is a difference. When you align yourself with spirit, you align yourself with that frequency; when you focus on the body, you align yourself with that frequency. What is that frequency? That frequency is one of separation. The body symbolizes separation, but ironically, it functions best at the frequency of love.

Heal the Mind, and the Body Follows

When you are at peace and completely align with love, your body will take care of itself. This is what we ask you to do as you go through these teachings: Focus on spirit and on healing the mind because in healing the mind, the body repairs itself, coming into a semblance of balance and health.

All sicknesses are of the mind. They seem to be in the body, but your unloving, fearful, hateful, judgmental, or self-loathing thoughts create them. These are the things that make your body sick. The body does not become sick on its own accord. We have said many times before and will repeat for those of you who have missed our previous teachings: Your body is a corpse. Yes, it is a corpse that is enlivened by spirit, by consciousness. Consciousness inhabits it, consciousness drives it, and consciousness motivates it. It is not motivated in and of itself.

So there are many (what you would call) scientific explanations in your society that counter this truth, but when you see a body that has "died," so to speak, the spirit has left it. You are actually seeing what the body is. It is an inanimate object that has no volition of its own other than the spirit contained within it. This is what you must consider to come to a complete understanding of what the body is. The body is a creation of the egoic consciousness; it is designed to be a demonstration of separation.

Now we approach the subject of love. Not only have you separated yourself from love by choosing separation, but you have also created this isolated and isolating thing called a body as part of your demonstration of it. Ironically, in using the body to find love, you cause some of your greatest pain. We must address this subject as it relates to love in your society because it is where you are the most out of accord with truth, where you are the most lost.

When you see and value yourself as a body, you are, in fact, siding with separation, and you will suffer because you focus on that which is a demonstration of separation. As you focus on something that demonstrates separation, you feel more separated, and your guidance system — that infallible, ever-communicating connection to the Divine — is going to say, "No, you are not on track." You mistake those negative feelings for an imperfect body. You look at your body and judge it because you feel bad, but your guidance system is actually saying that you are off track. You mistake those bad feelings as a correct assessment that your body must be faulty somehow because you feel bad, and so you amend the body. What you have to do is amend the mind. Many of you have eating problems, body dystrophies, and these sorts of things because you misinterpret the messages from your guidance system and you misuse the body.

The body is a communication device for experience only, and it is very good at that. But if you ask it to find love for you, it cannot because it is only an operating system, let us say. You are the one who puts the information in, who puts value on the body, and who decides whether it is acceptable. The body only does what you tell it; it only responds to what you do. It does not do anything on its own.

So you see the difficulty here. As you begin to focus on the body, you feel negative feelings, and you begin to hate the body. The ego-mind uses the body as one of its greatest weapons; not only does it tell you that the body is your greatest asset and that you should perfect it and use it as bait to catch love, but it also tells you that it is very fallible — it is frail, and it might die — so it cannot be counted on. You are given two opposing messages, completely contradictory information: The body is your god and will bring you what you want, but it will also fail you and cause you to lose everything that you have attained. This causes great emotional disruption in the mind, and you can see why this is so. To be told the very thing that is your god is going to fail you is a very confusing and crazy-making belief system, and that is the sign of the ego. It always tells you to chase something you cannot catch.

As you use the body incorrectly, you begin to feel bad, and this is where you need to reassess the use of the body in your search for love. True love is of the heart and the mind. That thing that you call carnal love is not love at all; it is a physical operation, like digestion. It is a physical, reproductive act, nothing more, and it is a very low-frequency act when approached from a purely physical point of view.

It is not sinful — there is no god judging you for how you use your body — but you feel feedback from your guidance system as you use the body to get certain things. If you use the body as bait to attract a partner and manipulate somebody, you will not feel good for very long, especially if these grasping needs come from fear or lack of self-love. This will not benefit you at all. We see many young women in your society use their bodies, in combination with drugs and alcohol, in an effort to find love. They use their beautiful, experiential machines incorrectly, and they cause themselves a great deal of suffering because their guidance systems, which are in alignment with love, give them very clear feedback that what they seek is not love. To become inebriated and then sleep with a stranger is not love, yet that is what some people call it. They will get another answer from their guidance system: A clear no will come through because they are far off track.

How do you get on track with the body and love? Well, it is not through casual or promiscuous sex; instead, it is through the meeting of minds. When you meet the mind of another being and you are openhearted and accepting, you connect in a meaningful way. You must understand that the body is nothing in and of itself; it is the mind and the heart of the other being that you are interested in. It is the mind and the heart of the other being that are intriguing for you, and the simple, physical lust of the animalistic self is not going to last long. This is one reason you see so many broken relationships in your world.

The spirit in you knows the truth: that love is held in the mind. This does not mean you cannot have a sexual relationship with the object of your desire; rather, it means you must fall in love with a person's heart and mind first. We ask those of you who seek love to look at the body not as bait or as ammunition for war but as an experiential device, a communication device between minds. In the meeting of minds, you will find the greatest joy. In the alignment of frequency, you will have the greatest joy, and when you align those things, the body follows along. You will have a meeting of minds followed by a meeting of bodies, and this is where true sacred sexual energy is released. When you have a meeting of minds and like-minded people who respect, love, and care for each other come together in the physical to share and exchange information and energy, you will find the lovemaking you want.

Now, there is a great deal of information related to sexual energy, sexuality, and the body, and we have, in fact, written a book addressing those issues, called *Making Love to God* [Light Technology Publishing, 2013], that takes you through all the machinations of love —sexual love, physical love, and spiritual love — and you can use it in combination with this book as a one-two punch, if you will. Using both, you can come to understand your journey through love, what love is, how it looks, and what it is for. We will say this: It is not the body that you love; it is the heart and mind of another being.

You have a very distorted view in your world, and it comes from focusing on the body. You have been taught to look at bodies, to value bodies, and to measure and judge bodies, and you have been sold a bill of goods. You constantly try to change the shape of your body when you should try to change the clarity of your mind. The clarity of your mind and the kindness of your heart will allow you to magnetize to you that which you seek. If you constantly focus on the size, shape, or quality of the body, you are only going to get that low-frequency kind of relationship magnetized to you.

Instead of being obsessed with your body, become obsessed with your mind. Become obsessed with your forgiveness practice, with your self-expression, and with being loving, and that will bring you everything you need.

You see, as you balance your mind, your body naturally follows. As you balance your mind, you will naturally want to go for a walk or a swim. These things are natural in the animal body that you inhabit, and they will rise to the surface of their own volition. You do not have to force yourself to do it. But when you are out of accord with love and with yourself, these things feel like disciplines and hard work. They are not hard work for the natural animals of your world. Look at a horse when it is given its freedom — or a cat or a dog — it will run and play and walk and sleep and eat (and never overeat, unless a human becomes involved).

Trust your natural instincts as you begin to clarify your mind and your heart and as you begin to let go of the future and focus yourself in this moment. You will see that the body will take care of itself. As you focus more on your own clarification, you will see miracles happen out in the world, and more love will show up in your world. It has to show up in the world because you are the creator, you are the one who is magnetizing it, so the more loving you are inside — in your mind and heart — toward yourself and others, the more love will show up on the outside.

Find Relief to Find Love

At this point, you likely feel somewhat overwhelmed by our messages, so we want to rein you back in to this moment. This moment is where all these things change. This moment is the only time when you have the ability to affect anything in your world. How do you know what to do in this moment? If you are looking for love, for a lover, or if you are single and perhaps sad about that, how do you find somebody? How do you begin that journey?

You must decide what feels best for you right now without the use of drugs or alcohol or food, the crutches humans in your society have been trained to use. When we ask you to choose the next thing that feels good to you, we want you to do that through the natural world. We want you to do that through your creativity or through nature, perhaps by going on a walk and taking some photographs. You might do it by writing or listening to music. You might do it by painting or meditating. There are many, many routes to find your relief or excitement.

Relief is what you look for when you feel stressed. You must take yourself on a journey from stress to peace before you can really discern what you would like to do. This is where most of you fall down in Western society. You are in a constant state of stress generated by your thoughts and ideas and beliefs, and fears arise from those thoughts and ideas and beliefs so that you cannot really acknowledge how you feel. You react to stress in the world based on your beliefs about the world.

This is a difficult time on your planet, as you are under the stresses of change and the disintegration of the old order. It will not stop. Yet there is a revolution afoot, and it is coming from millions and millions of people who are just like you, so in this moment, you have the power of a god. You have the power to choose what you focus on.

Throughout our teachings, we have suggested that you turn off your televisions. This is the first thing you can do to reduce the stress in your life. You know what is going on out there, and you do not need to have it thrust down your throat. It is always the same — the ego playing its game of death and destruction, war and famine. It does not matter whether you watch your television today or ten years ago or ten years in the future: It is always filled with negativity. Turn it off, and trust that taking negativity out of your life will help you.

Your society has designed television shows to involve you in emotional games. You become attached to the characters in shows and their emotional journeys because you do not have interesting lives of your own. We want to be honest here. Yes, it is harsh to hear those words, but the truth is a lot of you work in jobs you do not like and go home to uninteresting personal lives. So you turn on your television sets to tune into an emotional life.

When you turn away from an emotional life found on television, you make space for a real emotional life. But if you do not know how to negotiate your emotions (which most of you do not), then this sounds more frightening than festive. We want you to know that if you dedicate the time you spend watching television to educating yourself and to relaxing and exploring your inner world, you will begin to generate joy from within your mind. What is happening now for many of you is you are not able to make the shifts in your life that you want to make because you do not live the life you want to live, so your frequency is too low to get in touch with those higher levels of creativity and love and abundance. You must take these first steps as an act of faith that we know something you do not.

Pursue Christ Consciousness

Now, if you are feeling happy and joyful and you are at peace with your life, you are well along the way to finding love, and you will find it at the right time. You will find love when Spirit deems it appropriate for your consciousness evolution. If you are happy and peaceful at this moment as you read this book and look around your world feeling content with the way things are but disappointed that you do not have a partner, then you must trust that you do not have a partner yet because it is not the right time. We say, relax and explore yourselves more; there are things hidden in you yet that will benefit you, and perhaps you would not find them if you had a partner now.

You see, in your world, there are many habits and behaviors associated with coupledom that are detrimental to spiritual growth. Many habits and behaviors that have been deemed appropriate within relationships actually are very bad for spiritual evolution, so if you do not have a partner, perhaps you first have some things to uncover in your self-development. If you use this time to your benefit, you will raise your frequency and bring yourself to a higher realm where you can find the kind of partner that you would like.

We are not speaking here about the kind of partner that is just a body for you to hang out with or play with. We are speaking about sacred love relationships, relationships that are focused on and dedicated to the Divine. These are the love relationships we speak about. Why? Because that is the only kind of love that really exists. The "love" of the ego is built out of need and fear and desperation and loneliness. We are not speaking about that kind of relationship. We are speaking about the kind of love relationship that is generated from beings who know themselves inside and out and who have cultivated their inner selves, their creativity, and their self-expression in whatever form that takes. We have no preference, and Spirit has no preference. Spirit just wants you to express the unique you that has come to this Earth for a particular purpose.

If you do not yet feel that you have found your purpose, start to make new decisions today. We want you to begin to choose love today in each moment if you can.

One terrifying thought is that this life, in your body, is the only one you have. Life continues. Consciousness was before your birth and will continue after your death, and when you get in touch with this truth, you become much less fearful, much less jealous, and much less afraid of loss. This allows you to be more generous and more loving in your behavior.

The journey into love is about the pursuit of Christ consciousness. It is about the pursuit of divine love first and earthly love second, and to do that you must understand the truth of Jesus's teachings. Why? Because your society has contaminated those teachings, usurped them and made them into something hateful, something that causes suffering. Many of you have beliefs and ideas about good and evil and right and wrong, and they are not correct. You cannot bring your frequency up to the realm of love when you fear the afterlife, God, or the idea that you are a sinner. These are low frequency, fear-generating ideas, and you will not be able to raise yourself into the realm of love if you believe in them.

Be Present

Whoever and wherever you are, the work you must do is in this moment, and it is always in this moment. It is choosing what you focus on, listening to your guidance system, and quieting your mind. That is always the work, no matter how far along the path you are, and when you have gone a long way on the path, which is something you can look forward to, you will be given developments and interesting accomplishments as you are able to handle them.

You are all on your own journeys, your own unique paths, so do not try to emulate others; instead, understand that as you walk along your path to self knowledge and raise your frequency to the realm of love, you are going to have the most unique gifts bestowed on you. You are going to meet people you have not yet met, you are going to have loves you have not yet had, you are going to explore places and experiences you have not yet explored because you have not been ready for them.

So at this stage, we would like you to take a moment and completely and profoundly accept exactly where you are on your journey. Appreciate all the experiences you have had, forgive all the wrongs you believe have been done to you, take responsibility for your creative power, and accept that this is the moment that changes everything. In this moment of complete self-acceptance, self-appreciation, and self-love, you are an enlightened being. You lose your connection to your true self through self-loathing and hatred and judgment. In each moment, you have the opportunity to be that which you seek. You seek it in the future, but it is this present moment when you can be just who you are, can be kind to yourselves and those around you, and can listen to your inner guidance.

Go inside, and in a moment of peaceful self-appreciation, ask yourselves what it is you would like to add to your life that is not there. Listen to that inner voice, and write the answer in your journal. Tomorrow or, if you can, in this moment, do something to bring that thing into your life. If it is a partner and love that you seek, then continue reading, because this book is designed to help you accomplish that. It is designed to help you raise your frequency to the realm of love so that it must come to you.

CHAPTER 9

Align with Love to Find Happiness

THERE ARE MANY THINGS YOU LOVE IN THIS WORLD. YOU ARE PHYSICAL beings, spiritual beings, emotional beings, and mental beings, but most of all, you are loving beings. You were created from love. Your purpose is to love, and that is where your alignment must be for you to be happy.

We've said before that your definition of love is too narrow. Anything that brings you peace or joy or contentment or any positive emotional response that you have points to something you love. If you go for a walk and enjoy how the sunshine feels on your skin — you love it — that is alignment. If you cook a beautiful meal and then share it with friends or family, enjoying the tastes and the conversation and the nutrition, that is love and alignment. If you hold a new baby in your arms and wonder at the magnificence of life, that is love and alignment. In appreciating anything, aligning with anything, and enjoying anything, you are in alignment with love, and you are being love and loved. You must expand your definition of love to bring that special love into your life. If you are too narrow in your definition, you are not in alignment, and this is where most of you are when you seek a special love partner.

You Are Here to Experience

The special love relationship brings challenges because of your cultural conditioning. We do not want you to get depressed or disillusioned; we want you to understand the truth of the conditioning you have in your society. Your society says the special love relationship is the only thing that really counts, apart from your children or your relatives. Even then, the special relationship holds a paramount position in your psyche and in your culture. This is a form of separation, which is hard for you to understand because you think that is the place where you are going to find union or connection. Because you are conditioned to believe that the special relationship is more important than anything else, you are, in fact, missing many opportunities to raise your frequency. You are missing opportunities to love that would, in fact, bring you a more loving partner.

You see, when you are conditioned to love only one person, you search for that special one who is perfect, and you then separate yourself from every other person on the planet. Those beings are reflections of you. They are opportunities for you to come to know yourself, for you to love, and for you to explore your consciousness. When you limit your view of what love can be to the special love relationship, you limit your experiences and your self-understanding. This invites disillusionment to step into the special relationship after a while: You become very, very dissatisfied with such a narrow focus because you are meant to experience many things.

What happens in your special love relationships is disastrous, from our point of view, because you are so focused on getting everything you need from one particular person that you do not see the world around you. You are not open to many opportunities for self-expression, for experiencing beautiful communion with other beings. You shut out the world and shut down your heart. It is no coincidence that you have a high incidence of heart disease in your society: You are closed hearted. You are often hardhearted, and even within those special relationships, after the honeymoon period comes to an end, you close your heart. You harshly judge your partner, freely attacking him or her. At times, you hate your partner more than you hate anything else in the world. This happens because you are ignorant about what love is and you do not understand your guidance system.

Your guidance system (as we have said many, many times and will continue to say until it firmly implants in your mind) is in alignment with love, so when your partner dissatisfies you, you judge and separate from that person. How can one person satisfy you when you are meant to have many kinds of experiences, friendships, and relationships? How can you isolate yourself to one person and expect him or her to be the be-all and end-all for you? You receive negative feedback because you are out of alignment with love and your frequency dips below the frequency that love holds.

When you observe the world with love and you are open to speaking to other people and engaging in all kinds of different friendships and relationships — some based on conversation, some based on creativity, and some based on action — you will be much fuller. You will not be so needy, and you will have something to offer your special love relationship. You will not simply take.

When you isolate yourself in that special relationship, you feel empty because you do not get enough stimuli, let us say, from the world or enough opening into the world, so you become hungry for information and things. You try to find those things in your partner, but that person cannot give them to you. Your partner cannot give you the variety of conversation, environment, appreciation, and love that the entire world can give you.

We are not saying that you should not have a special love relationship; that is part and parcel of your separation experience. We *are* saying that we want you to understand how separation plays out in this relationship. As you study these teachings and come to understand what has happened to you, what you are experiencing, and what your emotional guidance system is telling you, you will hold less tightly to that special relationship and be much less fearful within it. As you become less fearful, open your heart to more experiences, honor yourself, and allow yourself to create and explore and expand, you will find that your special relationship will blossom and grow (not sexually necessarily, but that can happen if you so choose). It will expand because you are expanding. If you expand as the creator of everything you experience and in your appreciation of everything, your relationship will expand into the higher realm of love.

The Importance of Creativity and Self-Expression

We see many beings on your planet limit themselves because of archaic rules and regulations that have been applied to your male-female (or masculine and feminine) relationships. Many rules on your planet restrict women and cause them to be fearful. The patriarchal structure of your society has been long in the making, and the influences of the patriarchy are very strong. The women's liberation movement has stalled, we would say, because of the increased emphasis on the body and beauty in your mass media. Women have once again become imprisoned by rules and ideas that cause them to focus in a very limited way.

If your daughters were indoctrinated in creativity and self-expression instead of being over-sexualized, you would have a magnificent society. You would have a society that is far ahead of where it is now. You lose many of the great minds of your world because they are restricted and indoctrinated in obsessing over the physical structure of the body, and as we mentioned before, the more you focus on the body, the less happiness you find because the body is a demonstration of separation.

Remove Your Restrictions

The special love relationship as it exists in your society right now causes a lot of suffering. If you are in a relationship in which you feel imprisoned, look at where you are restricting yourself. You believe your partner wants you to be restricted, or you believe that the relationship requires this of you. Ask yourself, "Do I come home when I don't want to? Do I reject going to the pool for a swim when I wish I could? Do I watch a television show when I could go for a walk instead?" These are all unloving behaviors even though you might think that they are loving. They are restrictive. How do you know that? Your guidance system tells you that these behaviors are out of accord with it.

We suggest that you talk about these restrictions you feel with your partner. Many of you restrict yourselves because you were trained to by your parents, and your partner might not agree with you. He or she might actually be very surprised that you restrict yourself this way. This is how separation works. Your societal conditioning influences you, and this is especially true for women. Little girls are told to put aside their wants for others and to compromise and be nice when they would prefer to do something else. They grow up to be women who sacrifice themselves on the altar of marriage and wifedom and become very unhappy and disempowered. Your society is losing half of its energy in this way.

When you think about what love is, include yourself in the equation. Look at yourself and what your heart's desires are, and begin to honor those desires. Now, your ego consciousness and your training are going to speak up, and they will tell you that if you are honest, your relationship will crumble. Your relationship will end. What we are telling you is that if you do not honor yourself, your body is going to crumble, and your relationship will not thrive because you are sick and unhappy.

Being loving to yourself is being loving to your partner. Do not listen to the ego's thoughts and your conditioned ideas. How do you know which thoughts are which? You pay attention to how they make you feel. Does the thought of taking a walk after dinner enliven you and make you feel good, but you stop yourself because you have to do the dishes or your partner does not want to walk with you? These are the simple places where such thoughts and ideas play out. If the thought of a walk enlivens you and the thought of doing dishes does not, go for a walk. The dishes will still be there when you return home, and you will be invigorated and happy because you listened to your guidance system. On that walk, you might be inspired to take a photograph, or you might meet someone with whom you have a conversation. If you don't go, you might miss out on the simple pleasures of a creative life by restricting yourself in this way.

These are some simple ways you can begin to express love. You do not think of these things as love, but they are because they are in alignment with your guidance system. You are in alignment with love. As you align with your guidance system, the universe gently guides you to the path that is yours. You are guided to the path that is yours not by suffering and sacrifice but by joy and pleasure. Follow your bliss. You have heard this phrase, and it is true! When you follow your guidance system's simplest directions minute by minute, you are listening to Spirit show you the way to go.

Many of you are looking for great purpose in your life, for the perfect job or the perfect career or the perfect artistic expression, but the truth is, your destiny is contained within simple decisions. Are you going to do what you feel like doing in this moment, the thing that is going to make you happy? Or have you been trained to sacrifice yourself? Sacrifice is not required, and it is unloving. It is not required by Jesus, it is not required by God, and it is not required by anything in the universe. The universe is creative, self-expressive, and free, and you are too, but you have forgotten that you are, and you have been taught that you should not be, that freedom is evil somehow.

We are here to tell you the opposite. We are here to tell you that your freedom and your self-expression — being who you feel you want to be — is your right and your destiny, and as you begin to listen to those inklings, you will move further and further away from separation and closer and closer to love.

CHAPTER 10

Question Your Beliefs

THERE IS A LOT OF LOVE TO BE HAD FROM YOUR OBSERVATION OF THE world, and that really is the key to bringing your frequency up. Your frequency is generated by the thoughts and beliefs you hold, so we must keep our focus there for now. If we go into the actions and words of bodies, we look at effect and not at cause. What we want to remind you of here is that you cannot change the effect and have a lasting result. You can change the effect temporarily, which is what most of you do. You try to change your behavior or your words, but you do not really change anything of substance. You fix the result of an action that arises from belief.

Now we want to go into the basics of your behavior. Your behavior always arises because you think it is going to bring you what you want, so when you look at your life — your frequency, let us say — you might say, "If I want love but do not feel loving, I must not be experiencing love. I am not happy." Yet there are many behaviors, thoughts, words, and deeds that arise in you every day. Remember, thoughts come from beliefs, those thoughts cause feelings, and those feelings motivate you to do certain things. This is the basic principle of action we want you to understand. To restate, you have beliefs, they give rise to thoughts, thoughts give rise to feelings, and feelings give rise to action.

You act throughout the day. You get up and do certain things. You probably brush your teeth, wash your face, have a shower, wash your hair, and get dressed in certain clothes that you believe are appropriate for you to achieve the goals of your day. You might get dressed in an exercise outfit and go to the gym, you might get dressed in a suit and go to an office, or you might stay in your pajamas and remain in bed all day. All of these behaviors arise from the feelings generated by the thoughts that come from your beliefs.

So if your results — the effects of the cause — are not working for you, generally what transpires in the Western mind is to do the same thing but try harder. This is what you are taught to do. This behavior arises from a taught belief that if something does not work the first time, work harder for it; nothing comes easily, and without pain, there is no gain. These are beliefs your society indoctrinates in you. These beliefs cause you to push and to stress. These beliefs cause you to swim upstream instead of going with the flow of life. These beliefs work for the system that is in effect in your society because those in power want you to work hard — for them. Now, if you are unhappy at work, you think you must work harder to make yourself happier because you have been indoctrinated to believe that having more things that cost money will make you happier. You have been indoctrinated from birth in a consumer society, so you believe that if you own more things — a bigger house, a nicer car, more pairs of shoes — you will be happier.

Your Beliefs Limit You

We are trying to show you that many of your behaviors arise from beliefs that are not your own. They come from your church, your television, and your parents, who were also indoctrinated by their church and their television and on and on and on. Question the beliefs you hold in your mind. How do you know your beliefs need questioning? You know because you are not happy. You do things that do not make you happy, and you do not know why you are doing them. You believe you have to, but the motivation does not really come from joy. It does not come from your heart, and it does not come from your deepest, true self.

This is what most of you face in your Western world. You face lives that are not your own. You face mortgages and houses and families and cars and responsibilities and jobs that you have seemingly chosen, but once you begin to experience these things, many of you feel very unhappy, and you are confused by your unhappiness because you were told that doing these things would bring happiness. What we are doing with this work is asking you to question. Look beneath the form — the shiny car, the new shoes, the prestigious job, or the nice house. We ask you to look beneath the form and ask yourself how you feel.

How do you feel when you go to your job? How do you feel when you pay the mortgage? How do you feel when you drive your children to lessons all over town? How do you feel about being so busy? How do you feel about the person you live with? How do you feel about yourself? These are difficult questions for most of you because you have been taught not to ask them. Yes, you have been taught to override your feelings from the day of your birth, and now we are asking you to pay attention to your feelings.

This is a process. Just as many of you have been indoctrinated for decade after decade, you have been indoctrinated in these beliefs and structures. These structures arose from belief. The structures are your family, your home, your bank account, and your work, and they have energy of their own now. What we are asking you to do is to align with your true self, but to do that, you must go through a process of inquiry, of asking yourself, minute by minute, "Why am I doing this? Am I happy doing this? Is this what I want to continue doing?"

This is a very frightening place for the ego consciousness. Remember, you have come into separation to experience your own dreams, desires, and idols, or the things you worship. That is what you have been doing. You have come here, and you are allowed to do whatever you want, but what has happened is that the powers that be — the marketers, the hierarchies that rule your consumer society — have figured out how this separate consciousness works. They have, through much study and investment, figured out that there are basic fears and desires in the egoic consciousness that are very, very powerful, and they have spent a lot of time learning how to manipulate them. Many of you do not know you have been manipulated. Many of you do not know you have been indoctrinated to behave in certain ways for purposes that are not for your benefit but for someone else's.

It began in the early church when the hierarchical structures took over Jesus's teachings, which were about love and forgiveness and self-realization, and manipulated and edited those teachings so they could maintain control of people's money and thoughts. What they saw in Jesus was a powerful healer and transformer of minds, and they used his teachings for their own benefit. How do you know that they used these teachings for their own benefit? How do you know that these wonderful teachings were misconstrued and edited? You can tell by the fruits of those teachings. When Jesus taught, he healed, enlivened, and helped people. When the church took over his teachings, it began to punish and kill and restrict people. These are the fruits of its teachings.

So now we bring you to this time and place because this is where you must do your work. Look at the fruits of those teachings: environmental devastation; a warming planet; intense pollution; war; genocide; and epidemics of diseases, suicide, and drug and alcohol abuse. Many things are transpiring, and these are the fruits your system has produced.

Now, you might be in a part of the world where the system benefits you a little bit. Perhaps you are a Westerner, and you have a house, a car, a comfortable couch, and a refrigerator full of food, so you are not as stressed as other beings. But you are not as apart from this system as you believe you are; you are generating this system with all the other beings on this planet.

You are a creator god, and your beliefs, desires, wants, needs, and actions affect the collective, but because you are a separate consciousness, an egoic mind, this does not bother you much. It does not matter much because you believe in separation. Remember, you believe you are isolated from everybody else, and as soon as you close your front door, everything is fine. You have what you need.

Are you happy and healthy? Do you commune with people you love? If the answer to all these questions is yes, then you are in a good place, and you can continue what you are doing. However, there is another aspect to the experience you are having, and that is the grand projection.

Examine Your Motives

You only experience the parts of yourself that you accept, the parts of the mind that you can tolerate, and being incarnated in a physical body means you experience sickness and death (at some point) and many things that are difficult. That is the nature of this place, and we are here to help with the suffering that those things cause, but we must get to the heart of the matter, which is your mind and your beliefs. So if you are happy and content with your life and you are on a track that suits you, then we have to honor you. Your guidance system is saying that you are doing fine.

Let us turn to those who are not doing fine, who feel lonely or isolated from family or friends. Perhaps you don't have any friends or you are lonely and would like a partner. We ask you to inquire about what is going on beneath the form of your life. Why do you do what you are doing? What is motivating you? What motivates you is your belief in your beliefs! We ask you now to question your beliefs. As you go through your day, we would like you to question why you do what you are doing. Why do you go to the coffee shop and have a cup of coffee? Why do you dress the way you are dressed? Why do you drive what you drive? Why do you live where you live? Why do you have your hair the way you do? Why do you have makeup on or a very sharp, fancy suit? Why, why, why?

Now, this idea of questioning everything you do might seem overwhelming, but we do not expect you to do it all in one day. There is a training program that has been designed specifically for this process, and that is *A Course in Miracles*. The book was transmitted from Christ consciousness, and the voice is Jesus's. He has come through once again as a teacher and revolutionary, and we ask you to join in this revolution. This is a revolution of love, not a violent or an aggressive revolution. It is a revolution that requires some vigilance, discipline, and willingness. We ask you to be willing to question what you do. We ask you to be willing to ask yourself, "Can I keep doing this for as long as I need to do this, or am I going to break? Am I going to fall apart?" The teachings that are coming through this channel are designed to help you on that journey. They are designed to bring your beliefs to the surface, to get you to look and feel, and through this process, you will come to understand the belief system you hold.

These first steps of transforming your mind are acts of faith. They are acts of faith based on the material you are reading and the feeling coming from us. They are acts of faith based on the knowledge that what you've been doing is not working for you.

You must come to this basic understanding of yourself if what you believe and what you do based on those beliefs are not working for you. How are you going to change if you do not change the beliefs that cause the feelings that cause you to act? If you do not change your beliefs, you cannot change your behavior! You can discipline yourself for a little while to act differently, but you cannot really change yourself until you change the beliefs that motivate your actions.

We first asked you to accept yourself, and now we ask you to question yourself. These seem contradictory, but they are not. We want you to accept where you are, what is happening, and how you feel because until you accept something, you cannot change it. As long as you resist it or deny it or wish it were other, you are not able to change it. You must first accept it, then look at it, and then question it. Begin to question. However, questioning beliefs with an untrained and confused mind is very difficult. That is why we recommend you do the lessons of *A Course in Miracles*.

What you do in those 365 days is temporarily hand over to love, to Christ consciousness, your decision-making mind and ask for help. You say, "I don't like the fruits of this tree. They are bitter fruits, and I don't want to eat them anymore, but I can't change them because I planted the seeds of this bitter tree. I need help. I need a higher mind and a higher frequency to guide me into the higher realms, into the realm of love, and I am willing to try something different because I know that the harder I work at what I believe in, the worse it gets."

Our quest is to get you to be willing to entertain the idea that perhaps something or someone somewhere knows more than you do, knows something more than that which you hold in your conditioned mind at this time.

CHAPTER 11

Implement Healthy Routines

LET US CONTINUE OUR DISCUSSION OF LOVE. WE ADDRESS PARENTS and soon-to-be parents now because you are very powerful influences on your children's lives. For those of you who have children already, know that whatever has transpired between you and your children up to this point, you are not responsible for any pain or distortion you have caused in their emotions and minds. You were ignorant of the actions you took and perhaps unaware of any damage that was done.

In this experience in separation, many errors are made. This is where your pain comes from. Your errors come from your misunderstandings, your "misteachings," your misguided-ness, and your ignorance. So we want you to make this day a new day. We want you to pay attention to where you lead your children. We want you to think about what you teach your children and what you ask them to do. Become aware of when you override their guidance system. Perhaps you ask them to eat something they do not want to eat, or you tell them to eat more when they are already satisfied. Perhaps you buy them candy or sweet treats that are bad for their bodies. These are areas where you can begin to shift.

Now, you must do your work first before you can become a better parent who can teach children something new. You first must work on yourself, so do not make your children your project instead of you! You are your project; you are the one who is uncovering your feelings, your frustrations, and your true desires. Your children will see and feel and witness those changes happening in you, and if you have a difficult or fractious relationship with them, you will see some very good shifts happen and where you have caused some of the problems.

Making such a shift is difficult for parents in this society because they have been deeply indoctrinated in what a good parent is. They have been deeply indoctrinated in how to control and change their children and in what makes a good child. These are all cultural teachings and, generally speaking (yes, we are generalizing here because we could write an entire book about children, and perhaps we will at some point), we want you to know that most things you have been taught about parenting are incorrect.

Honor Your Children

There are some advanced and modern parents out there who honor their children. Your children are not yours; they have come through you. Many chose their parents for genetic purposes only and tolerate living under their thumbs, so to speak. We would like you to truly love your children. What does this mean? Well, it does not mean heaping your limiting ideas and thoughts on them and trying to enforce them. It does not mean you try to limit them to fit into the box of a future you imagine for them in a job or a marriage or whatever.

Pay attention to what your children ask for. They are closer to Spirit than you, they have not been as indoctrinated as you, and they are wiser than you. Yes, they are wiser than you, depending on how much indoctrination has been inflicted on them, but because you have read this book to this point, we assume you are somewhat of an awakened parent. You would not be reading this material if you were not.

Honor your children. See them as your equals, for they are that, and some of them are incredibly wise beings who have come through to assist this planet in its transformation. They knew you would need help, so they volunteered to come into physicality to help you with your transition, but they are also being conditioned. Some of the starseed children who have come to assist by bringing their wisdom and their creativity to this plane unfortunately have been victims of some of your medications and of your corporal punishments because they are nonconformists. They will not want to do what traditional society wants them to do.

If you have a child who causes you some consternation, who refuses to conform to school and to the standards and schedules and behaviors that you think will help him or her fit into society, we ask you to lighten up on that child a little bit. You will have to play two hands of cards here. First, begin to truly parent, which means providing what that child needs to thrive, not what you need to feel as if you are a good parent. You will also have to play your own hand, which means listening to your feelings, thoughts, ideas, and the prescriptions and explanations we have laid out for you to readdress and reconfigure how you parent.

Help Your Children Move Away from Violence

There are many examples of children acting out or causing difficulty or being disruptive in your world, and we could go into many examples of that, but here we go into the general principles so that you can transfer and apply them to many different areas.

First, if your children watch violent television, begin a dialogue with them about that. Some of you have set up very bad habits by allowing your children to watch what they want, and they are being programmed for war and violence and hatred; do not doubt this. This is why your society looks the way it does. You have been programmed for war; and television, movies, and video games are some vehicles that allow this to happen. We understand that this is a Pandora's box for many of you because your children are deeply drawn to these activities. Why? Because this is part of the ego's separation consciousness, and when you are unaware that it is being fed, it feels very good. This is why television shows and movies focus on death and murder: The ego loves it. It loves death, attack, and separation. But as a parent now waking up to these realities, you must begin to exert some influence.

If your children have some extremely violent videos games, lovingly put your foot down and clearly explain why. Talk to your children about war and its costs. Talk to your children about the creative aspects of their minds. Talk to your children about their emotional guidance systems, and perhaps negotiate to trade those extremely violent games for some new games that focus on sports or some more creative outlet.

Now, this is going to be a difficult journey for you and your children because habits have been set up, so we want you to first begin to change their minds. Explain how creation works and that what people focus on becomes magnified out in the world. Go into some basic descriptions of how creation works, which will be very good for you because you will have to study up on that to answer some of the questions they will have. If you have smaller children, you need to monitor what they watch, and in an ideal world, they would not watch anything at all except perhaps nature documentaries. Disney shows are not free from programming and indoctrination that limit children, so do not assume they are all sweetness and light. They are not. Focus on creative and outside physical activities for your children. Focus on nature. Do not overschedule them; instead allow them free time to get bored. Unplug the cable to limit what they can watch, and you too will go through television withdrawal.

This is the most important front-line defense against limiting, consumer-centered, war-filled, and fearful ideas that come through the television. This is an important responsibility for you as a parent, but you can do it over several months so that you do not jar your children's minds. Remember, they have become indoctrinated in certain habits, and they have become habituated to certain images and frequencies. As you begin to shift, they will shift too. Slowly but surely exert some of your parental influence through your actions.

For example, instead of allowing them to sit around and watch television on a weekend day, you can round them up and take them to a park or go skiing. Now, most parents will say, "It's expensive to take my children out because they want 'this' and they want 'that.'" Yes, they do want "this" and "that" because they have been trained to want. This is part of the retraining program.

Trust us — as you shift yourself, these things will naturally flow back to you because you are the projector of your world and your children are actors in your play. So as you become more focused on love, as you turn off your violent television, as you go out more, and as you become more creative, you set a wonderful demonstration of love. Yes, this is all love related. If you want your children to be happy and healthy and to have good love relationships — and you want to have good love relationships with your children — then these are the things you need to integrate into your world.

The New World Will Have Different Needs

This is about love. This is about finding the great love of your life, which, of course, is you. And for your children? You want them to be able to explore their own feelings, inner worlds, creativity, and magnificence. As long as the other things go on, you are not giving your children that which they need for the new world.

The new world is not going to look like the old world. The new world will not want automatons and consumers and people who can sit at their desks for ten hours a day. It is going to need creative, innovative, courageous, fit, and healthy people to thrive, so that is the gauntlet we throw at your feet right now. We are telling you point blank that the future world your children will be in is not going to look like this one. It is not going to be the same.

Understand that you are giving your children a great gift by freeing them from these systems. You are giving them love by countering these systems even though you will meet some resistance in the beginning. They will actually become happier because the things that limit them and the violent things they watch do not make them happy. Those things make them sad, further immersed in separation, and further away from love. Therefore, these are great gifts you can bestow on your little ones.

We recommend you entertain the idea of cutting back on vaccinations for small children. You have the right to vaccinate them less frequently, and you have the right to vaccinate them in smaller quantities. We would like you to step up to the plate here for your children, do some research about the diseases that are being vaccinated against, and talk to your doctor about reducing the frequency and beginning the system of vaccination later on.

The child's immune system needs to have some experience of its own, not just the indoctrination from outside, from a system that is sickness based, not health based. So these are some of the things that you can do for your children.

The rules and regulations of your society are becoming more and more stringent as it relates to vaccines, so we suggest you take the slow and steady route, postponing those first injections and talking to your doctor about only giving them one at a time so that your child's body can react and cope with the influx of foreign material in a kind and measured way.

We do not want to overwhelm you. We know this is a lot of information, and it can be difficult for you, but once again we remind you that these changes can be made over months or even a year or two. Another thing that we would like you to pay attention to — and it is very, very important — is the food your children eat. Your frequency and your emotions are greatly influenced by your food, so please keep the foods for your children as healthy as possible. Restrict meat consumption considerably. They do not need it. If you would like to have meat, have it once or twice a week, and make sure it is organic and humanely raised. You could source that out on a wonderful road trip to a country location near you. See whether you can find a farmer who organically raises livestock, and take your family on an exploratory journey to find healthy sources for food. Eliminate the boxes and the cartons and the food that can sit on a shelf for weeks and weeks without going bad. That tells you it is not alive. Live food rots and must be refrigerated.

Be Measured in Making Changes

Do not stress yourself out when making these transformations. You must be loving to yourself, so do it when you are inspired and remain focused on the goal, which is getting all of your frequencies closer to love. We remind you that these are not acts of discipline; these are acts of love. To feed your children healthy food and to be concerned about their emotional and mental well-being is loving and will create more loving relationships and healthier bodies for them so that they can enjoy their experience here on the physical plane.

Do not force these things on your children. Know they have come onto this plane at this time because they knew what they were coming into. They will be very happy to have a dialogue with you about these principles. They will recognize these principles and respond positively to the discussions because they knew what they were coming into, and they would not be here if they were not prepared to do the work required for the new world to come into being.

Set your sights high, but be gentle. Set your goal on love, but understand that you have been confused and have set up some systems that are not in your children's best interests. There are many, many things you can do in a day that are loving or unloving. The choice is yours, but be aware as a parent. Be awake enough to make good decisions. How will you know? You will know by how you feel. When you are aware and present as you walk along the aisles of food, you will begin to feel what is good and what is not good. You will get internal messages from your guidance system, which is Spirit speaking to you. Remember, your guidance system is in alignment with love, and it is connected to your guides and teachers. As you become more aware of it, as you listen to it more and you begin to discern where you are conditioned and where you are free, you will have very clear guidance, so you do not need to be confused.

You have probably already had clear guidance. You have been upset about your children watching violence and eating bad food, but somehow these things have made it into your house. Stand up for the principles of love as your right, but do it gently, do it kindly, and do it over a period of time so that you do not scare your children and cause them difficulty. These indoctrinations and routines and habits have been set up over quite some time, and it will take time to undo them.

You are an aware, intelligent, and love-focused being, and you will be able to beautifully and gracefully master this transformation, this frequency elevation toward love, with your wonderfully inventive and creative mind.

CHAPTER 12

The Choice Is Yours

THE WORLD YOU ARE LOOKING AT NOW IS THE CONSEQUENCE OF THE beliefs you have been holding. Yes, you as an individual are creating every second of every day. Your parents created every second of every day, and your grandparents created every second of every day, and on and on. Generation after generation of beings who have been removed from their true power have created a system that usurps your power because you did not own it. You must remember that this is a reflective world, and these oppressive systems, these multinational corporations and warring, deceptive governments are the result of your creations! You must understand this so that you do not attack anybody; this is how the ego works.

When you attack, you remain weak and separated, and this is the irony of it all. The powers that be, the hierarchies that have been in charge of your world for a very long time, have known this all along. They constantly keep you trained into a state of attack and judgment and fear. Why? Because that keeps you in a low frequency and means you are stuck in the material, physical world where you are afraid of death and are very ego driven. That is what all the commercials about bodies and so on propagate in your mind. Television shows and news programs about death are all ego-strengthening methods to keep you very malleable and small.

Those of you who are innocents (and there are many of you out there) look at the world and believe your government is working for your best interests, the television stations are independent, and programming is chosen for many different reasons. But we are here to lay it on the line for you because we have to. We have to let you know what is happening on your planet's surface, and it is not what it seems to be. It is a grand conspiracy; a grand, multileveled, multifaceted operation to keep frequency low and to allow beings who thrive on taking to maintain control. This is why your system looks as distorted as it does. This is why there are peace-loving populations ruled by war-mongering governments that do not listen to what the people want.

Initiate a Revolution of the Mind

A revolution has to rise from the grass roots, and it has to be a revolution that takes place in your minds because your minds are being used to keep this system going. It is a sad story for you to hear, but it is the truth, and it is anything but love. We are writing this book so that you can begin to understand what is happening in your world. You can begin to understand and see when you are unloving, when you lack in love, and when you are separated from the mind of what you call God, or All That Is. In that understanding, you will begin to see the manipulations and orchestrations that are happening in your society.

Why is consumerism rife around the planet? It is pushed because the powers that be know that when people focus on the material, they do not focus on the spiritual. If you focus on the spiritual, you become powerful, influential, and knowledgeable, and you tap into wisdom, love, and truth. These systems cannot survive if you become spiritual, and this is what we are depending on you to do.

You have a choice. This is your world, and you get to live in the results of your own mind and see the outcome of your creation, so the kind of world and family and body experience you have is entirely up to you. We are not in the physical realm as you are; we have risen above it and are outside it, so we do not suffer the way you do. We want you to truly grasp why you suffer and how it comes about. This knowledge that we and Jesus are bringing through about love and forgiveness and openheartedness and defenselessness is the opposite of what you have been trained in, and it is a challenge to learn; there is no doubt about it. These concepts are a challenge because you have been told, generation after generation, that if you practice them, you will be weak, you will be taken advantage of, or you will be possessed! Trust us, these stories have been used to keep you away from Spirit and from being kind, openhearted, and generous because if you are hateful, fearful, and judgmental, your powers are no threat to the powers that rule your world!

For some of you, this is disconcerting because you read these books seeking peace and spiritual enlightenment from what is a very narrow point of view, the point of view that has been allowed on your planet. This universe you live in is far more complex than you know, dear ones. There are many cultures and civilizations on other worlds, and there are many, many beings of high consciousness you would not consider Spirit but rather extraterrestrial beings! These beings have your welfare, your growth, and your spiritual education as their goal because they are wise and loving, and they are tapped in, or tuned into, the love frequency.

When you tune into the love frequency, you can see suffering and cannot tolerate it because you know it is a choice. You are making the choice to suffer unknowingly and unwittingly, and you have been trained to do so. We are here to bring that truth to light and to encourage you to do this personal internal journey to transform your world. It goes against all the rules you have been taught and all the philosophies your world has been impregnated with, but it is the truth. You are all creators of these low-frequency events because you have unwittingly handed over your power to beings who do not have your best interests at heart. They use their knowledge of the egoic consciousness to get the power and influence and money they want. If you are an environmentalist, a peace lover, or simply someone who cares about children, family, and the world, this is the time to take responsibility for your thoughts, to turn off your televisions, and to begin reeducating your mind.

We are not here to scare you; your governments do that well enough. We are here to empower you, and Jesus, in his original teaching on this planet, was here to empower you as well. He has returned to teach those principles of love, higher mind, and higher consciousness through this particular being. So the next part of this book is through him. He will bring his teachings of love into this text so that you can have another level of appreciation for the care and consideration that Spirit has for you on this planet.

We are Ananda. We are your teachers, your friends, and your fellow journeyers on this most magnificent, creative journey and exploration of consciousness that you call life. We have had a wonderful time working on this book. Reread these chapters, and practice and follow these prescriptions. Implement them in your life. As you open your minds to truth and discipline them to focus on love, you will have wonderful, wonderful new experiences, and you won't stay in the state in which you find yourselves now.

For many of you, reading these texts feels overwhelming because you imagine you will have to add all this to the chores you already have, but that is not so. Your life is going to drastically change as you change your mind. It must because you are the projector and creator of everything, and as you align with love, as you forgive and discipline yourself, you will see reflections of love in your world that come more and more frequently, closer and closer, because you are demonstrating that frequency. You are the greatest magnet in the universe; you are the human mind focused on love, and that will bring love to you.

There are more stories. Next, Jesus elaborates on the principles and goes more deeply into some of these subjects. We leave you now and ask you to continue reading. Thank you for allowing us into your consciousness, and we will meet you there again soon.

PART 2

Put Love into Action
Jesus

CHAPTER 13

Forgiveness Demonstrates Love

I AM THE ONE YOU KNOW AS JESUS, AND THIS EXPLORATION OF LOVE IS my work. It has always been and continues to be my work. The stories you have heard about me are all wrong, and of course I addressed that in the book *Jesus: My Autobiography*, so you might have a firm footing in these teachings already. Now I want you to think about love specifically. I want you to think about how to love, what love is, and what it represents in your mind. You need to clarify your beliefs about love.

This book is designed to expand your definition of love, and first and foremost, it is about forgiveness, which is how you demonstrate your understanding of love. "How does this work?" you ask yourself. "How does forgiveness demonstrate love other than in the simple obvious way that it is a nice thing to do?" If you understand that this world is a projection of your mind and that what you see "out there" arises from within you, then attacking that attacks you. To attack others is to attack yourself and is therefore the most unloving act you can perpetrate on yourself.

It is a complete shift in consciousness, a complete transformation of your mind, that I ask you to make here, and the founding principle is this: The world you see arises in your mind. All the feelings you have arise within your mind. All your suffering arises within your mind. The basic tenant of love is not to attack the world because you would be attacking a part of your mind that you are unaware of. You attack that which arises from you, so it causes great fear within you to attack another because the mind is whole. The mind is integrated even though you are unaware of it.

When you attack that which is outside you or that which you believe is outside you, you are, in fact, attacking yourself, so anxiety and guilt and fear arise in the mind. One of the great causes of individual suffering is the idea of constant judgment of the "outer" inadvertently creating these feelings of guilt and shame and anxiety. Many anxiety disorders, this thing you call depression, and suicidal thoughts come when you inadvertently attack yourself because you do not understand the structure of the mind. There is a collective consciousness — a collective soul, if you will — that you are a part of, and it is important that you begin to truly understand this and comprehend it in the deepest parts of your mind.

Most of you have no idea what is going on in your consciousness other than a lot of thoughts that drive you crazy. That is a simple way most of you would describe your inner world. But that crazy mind is creating, and yes, it is creating a crazy world. You must take this to heart. The crazy, hateful, anxiety-inducing, fearful, mistrustful, jealous, rage-filled, and vicious thoughts are all creative. And the more strongly you feel them, the more creative they are.

On those nights when you are awake churning with resentment about somebody, entertaining fear about money, or getting sick (or sicker) and not able to continue your duties, those thoughts create. They come to you in forms and shapes and experiences and people of a like frequency. That is what happens to you. If you are constantly in a state of stress, anxiety, and worry and your mind is churning, churning, churning, then that is the world you experience: a churning, upset, and anxiety-inducing world. And yes, that is exactly what you are seeing now!

These teachings are very important not only in reducing your stressful thoughts and suffering but also in transforming this world that has gone out of control. The world has gone out of control because the collective mind has gone out of control, and these teachings are coming through now because it is time to rally as a collective to discuss these thoughts and ideas so that you have some support and are not alone in a desert, wondering whether you have gone crazy.

There is a story about me in a desert. I was infused with love and truth and the mind of what you call God, and I battled it with my ego mind.

That is exactly what took place, and you do not want to have that experience, so you must find like-minded souls who will go on this journey or are on it already.

A Course in Miracles has been on this Earth plane for some time now, and there are groups all over the place — many, many gatherings of people — who have studied and are studying this material. There are videos and teachings online, and it is free and available to you, so you do not need to have any money to do this. You do not need to have deep pockets to participate in this teaching, but you must put some effort into it, the same effort that has gone into indoctrinating you in fear. There has been a lot of effort to indoctrinate you in fear, and that has gone on for thousands of years, so this is no small task we set for you here. This is not a small assignment you are being given. You are being asked to retrain your mind completely, and you know how much effort has been put into training it so far.

Do this for your health and peace of mind. Do this for your children because they will inherit the world you are creating in this moment with your anxious or your peaceful thoughts. And do it for love's sake.

You are all made of love, from love, for love, and all that is wrong in your world is that you are out of alignment with love. As I journey into this subject with you, I ask you to begin the lessons of that text. That text is a sacred, divinely inspired document that came through several decades ago, and it is designed to do this work, systematically, kindly, lovingly, and in a way that will not disrupt your mind and your sanity.

You cannot fix a disordered mind with the same mind. This is a basic principle of sanity: An insane person cannot make him- or herself sane, and most of you are technically insane. It is not an insult; it is merely an observation. When you look at your world, you see an outside representation of an interior condition. As you begin the second part of this book, I bring forth more teachings that will assist you in understanding your mind and your relationship to love.

In Forgiveness, You Find Strength

As we move forward on this journey into love, we cover many different topics from my point of view. My point of view is quite different from any other being's point of view because of the history and experiences I have had. In your world, the journey I went on is a unique one, and that is why this version of reality is so important. The version of reality that each of you lives in is uniquely your own because of your lenses of perception, which are tainted. Each lens of perception that you have is from the past, from experiences you have had and kept with you. These unforgiven experiences limit your ability to see the truth. They cloud your ability to experience with clarity and with love. Love is clear, has no resentments, and holds no grievances, so when you have these lenses of perception from the past, you do not see clearly and cannot love clearly. This is where forgiveness comes in.

Each time you forgive, each time you let something go, your perception becomes clearer and clearer, and the lenses fall away from your vision. As the lenses fall away, and your emotions calm down. You discover that your volatility and emotionality are triggered by the untrue ideas in your mind, and you realize the distortion these lenses cause in the world you see.

Beings who completely clarify their minds will not react to the world as if it is a separate thing; they will respond to the world knowing that it arises from their consciousnesses, and they will be clear and loving. So your journey into love is one of clarification. Your journey into love is one of cleansing, one of letting go of these distorting lenses of perception.

That is what I did in my life; however, it was the culmination of many incarnations, not that one only. This is how your limited vision does not assist you. You think you have one life only, and you must defend it to the death. How ironic is that?

You must become defenseless; you must become clear and be able to love absolutely, achieving that which you call enlightenment. Now, many of you are nowhere near enlightenment; you are, in fact, immersed in distorted ideas and visions that you look through. Know that behind those lenses is an unaltered soul, a soul that is connected to love, is completely connected to All That Is, and is eternal. As lens after lens distorts your vision and you become more and more separate from the truth because of the past experiences you have not let go of, you become less and less clear and less and less able to love. We are on the journey of removing these lenses so that you are not volatile and emotional.

This is an interesting aspect of the egoic consciousness. You have been told that feeling emotions is what makes you human, and this is true in some ways, but feeling reckless, violent, aggressive, or terrified emotions does not make you human; it makes you dangerous and unable to love. The volatility of the ego comes from fear, not from strength. The peace of the loving mind is the ultimate in power because it means you are connected to the divine will, and when you are connected to the divine will, you have access to all the power of the universe, to all the creativity of the human mind aligned with the divine mind, and that is God's will for you.

Now, some of this language is distressing for you because of its history, so this is also something you must forgive. For many of you, *A Course in Miracles* is difficult because the words "God," "Jesus," and "church" are used. These are all aspects of forgiveness that you must explore. For many of you, these are the greatest challenges of *A Course in Miracles* because you hold resentments against me, against God, and against the church, and as long as you hold those resentments, you cannot clearly hear the wisdom that is contained within the voice of that book. It is my voice, and my voice comes only from love and teaches only peace, but until you have forgiven me for what has been done in my name by other beings, you will not be able to clearly listen to those words.

So if you tried to read *A Course in Miracles* but resented the language, come back and do your forgiveness work with the words. Words are only words, lines on a page. What they bring up in you is *in you*, not in the words. As this rage about the violence that has been done in my name comes up, ask me to help you clarify and remove that lens of misperception from your mind because it keeps you in the material world and away from love, and our purpose is to return you whole and complete to that original state of being, the unaltered soul that you are. As you step through the language, you might have triggers. Feminists in the group might be angry that the words "he," "father," and "son" are used. Your resentments of these words are in you, and you must forgive them. In forgiving the words, you reclaim your feminine connection to the Divine. You will forgive your brothers and your fathers and your gods for all the violence perpetrated on women, and it will make you strong and clear and loving. It will bring you back to your truth and to your center. As long as you resent men for what they have done to you and resent me for what I have been forced to represent, you will remain in a separate and powerless state.

Part of the female reclamation of power is in forgiving men for what they have done to women. This is a difficult journey for the sisters in this congregation, but in forgiving men for what they have done and the church for what it has done, you will become more empowered, and you will reclaim the great, aligned spirit you are. So deal with your resentments with the language in *A Course in Miracles*. Bring up those thoughts and ideas that make you angry.

Whether those thoughts are of a father who abused or overpowered you or a husband who hurt or attacked you in some way, these are your forgiveness practices now, and they are powerful ones. Half of the world is being resented and hated and kept away from love.

That is your gift to the world now: to forgive the men, to forgive the church, and to forgive me for the sins that I have not committed. You are a united being in truth, but you believe you are separate. Women, you believe you are weak not because you are but because you are taught you are. The grandiosity perpetrated on women in patriarchal societies makes you feel less than, and that is yours to own. You must begin to reclaim your power, and ironically enough, it will be found in forgiving those who are your victimizers, in forgiving those who hurt you.

CHAPTER 14

The Only True Actions

THERE ARE MANY FORMS OF LACK OF LOVE IN YOUR SOCIETY. YOU CAN list hatred or sinning or jealousy or fear or domination or war, but they are all of the same origin, and that is a lack of love. Once you begin to truly comprehend that these variations on a theme the ego mind is very clever at creating are meaningless and that there is only one solution to all of the problems on your planet, life becomes much simpler. Everything you experience as suffering is a lack of love, a distortion in your ability to see clearly, and that is the lens we referred to in the previous chapter.

When you begin to clearly focus on and comprehend the truth, you discover that there are only two actions: a call for love and a response of love. These are the only two actions in the world, as there are only two conditions: the presence of love or the lack of love. There is a call for love or an act of love. These are the only things that you ever witness. You give them many names, many forms, but that is all that happens in your world.

Once you stop being confused about the complications and complexities of life, you begin to ask yourself, "What is happening in this situation? Is it a lack of love or an act of love?" When a child is lying on the floor crying, screaming in a tantrum, that is clearly not an act of love, but it is a call for love, so you take love to that situation. You do not attack or smack or judge or hate or wish that child away. You bring love to the situation. You might sit quietly next to the child, without judgment and with peace and love in your heart, and wait for him or her to calm down. Or you might gently soothe the child, stroke his or her hair, or offer some kind words. These are some examples of appropriately responding with love to a situation that clearly demonstrates a lack of love.

When you are sick and you body hurts, are you experiencing an act of love or a lack of love? It is a lack of love. Look at your behavior as it relates to your body not only in the physical acts that you engage in but also the thoughts you have about it and the words you speak to yourself or others about it. This is clearly a lack of love, so you must look at your experience and say, "Ah, how can I add love to this mix? How am I feeding my body? What stories am I telling about my body? What am I asking of my body? Are these loving things? Are these kind things? Or do these lack love?"

Life becomes very simple when you look to simple principles, and the same goes for your personal relationships. When you are in a relationship, whether it is sexual or platonic, if there is friction or a disagreement or simply annoyance, take time to ask yourself, "Is this an act of love or a call for love?"

Imagine your loved one stays out drinking late and is hung-over the next day. If you are angry with that person, you are not adding love to the lack of love; instead, you are adding anger to the lack of love, which is a continued lack of love, an increased lack of love, or deprivation. But if you add love to the mix by taking that person a drink of cold water and asking how he or she feels, perhaps you can help that person feel a little better. You add love. Your ego will not want to do that. It will say, "If I help heal this person after a bender, I am supporting his (or her) alcoholism." In the ego's world, that would be a true statement. You do not help people when they are in pain. You let them feel it, you let them suffer, and you leave them alone to die or to drink themselves into oblivion. But Spirit would not do that; Spirit would genuinely and authentically bring love to the mix and keep offering it.

Sacrifice Is Unnecessary

We do not want you to think that loving somebody means you have to allow him or her to abuse you. Loving somebody does not mean you give up your life for that person; it means when you are in that person's presence, you are loving. When that person comes to mind, you send loving thoughts. It does not mean you do not live your own life. There have been some great distortions in the history of the teachings around my life. The church used my life as a demonstration of suffering and sacrifice, and that was not what it was at all.

The body was meaningless to me. I mastered the physical world by the time I was hung on that cross, and it was a statement of my immortality, not a testament to my weakness or my physicality in any way, shape, or form. I knew I could make a new body, that I was not body dependent, so it was not a sacrifice for me at all. It was a demonstration of my lack of belief in the body, in fact. But the church took those teachings and distorted them and twisted them, as it did with many things I spoke about and demonstrated. It took the parts that worked in its favor, the parts that helped it overcome peoples' wills and manipulate their feelings. This has been long in the making in your society. You have been taught these foundational lessons on threat of death over millennia. We want you to know these ideas of suffering and sacrifice are incorrect.

Love does not sacrifice. In the present moment, it is kind. In the present moment, it offers companionship or some form of healing energy or thought, but it does not sacrifice. It does not give up its own life, and this is where you have become confused in your society. You think that if you are, say, married to an alcoholic, you must stay with that person and suffer. That is not the case at all. You must be loving to yourself and others, and that is always an inclusive statement. You must love yourself. Does living with that person make you happy? Does living with that person bring you joy? Does living with that person fulfill you? If yes, then continue on, but if living with that person is not working for you, if living with that person does not make you feel good, then you do not have to remain there. You are a being of free will and free choice, and you are allowed to do whatever you wish with your life and experience the consequences, both good and bad, of that creative expression.

The teachings of the church will tell you to sacrifice and stay and punish yourself and suffer with that person. Love does not do those things! Love offers kindness in the moment, a peaceful mind, a peaceful heart, and open hands, but it does not sacrifice itself.

Find Where You Lack Love

Look at your life to see where there is a lack of love. How do you know there is a lack of love? There is suffering. There is suffering when there is an absence of love because you are meant to be in the frequency of love and aligned with that frequency. So if you have a marriage that is on the rocks, there is a lack of love there. If there is fighting or disagreement or fractious behavior or hateful words, your responsibility there is to make a choice. If you would like to try to save the marriage, then you must add love to the mix, and that means with you first! How can you love yourself more? When you are loved, healthy, and looking after yourself, you have much more to offer somebody else. You are not deprived, you are not sacrificing, and you are not suffering. So in that circumstance, add love first to yourself, and as you love yourself more, you will have more love to give others.

If you look at your work and find you are suffering there, you are not satisfied, or you do not feel you can continue doing it, then you must add love to the mix. What does it look like in that circumstance? Add love as it relates to your education, or perhaps seek to do more of that which you love to find out about what you love. Honor yourself, and say, "If I have to spend this many hours each week doing something, I am going to do something that I love." Begin to honor yourself in that way.

Many of you are taught unloving things about yourselves. You are told you lack personal power, you lack education, or you lack intelligence, and you feel you do not deserve better, so you do not ask yourself for better. That is a lack of love.

Begin to add love to your work environment. Add love where you are even when you do not like your job. Start by adding love to the environment because if you are shut down, closed off, or hateful at this job, you are going to get more of the same. But if you want to change your job, have a better time, or enliven your employment, then bring more love immediately, even to that place that you do not wish to work at anymore. You will then raise your frequency and bring a light into that place, and in that loving act, you will bring more love and better work to you. You will bring more nice opportunities to you.

These are some ways to discern the difference between love and a call for love. Life is very, very simple. In this moment, you are in a loving place, which means you are at peace, you are happy, and you are doing what you want. Or you are in an unhappy place, an unloving place, a place that lacks love. If you are unhappy in this moment, ask yourself what you could give to the circumstance that you are not giving now. Are your arms folded and your eyes down? Are you refusing to participate? Are you resentful or angry? These are your choices. If you are not giving love, you cannot feel love. It is very simple. You will blame the situation, but it may very well be that you are the problem.

This is not the way you are used to looking at the world. You are used to looking at the world as an objective reality that is the problem, but you are part and parcel of your reality. You create it, you interpret it, and you experience it. It is all happening within you, and you are the one that must decide: Is this an act of love or a call for love? That is all there is in the world. Determining which is the only decision you ever have to make.

We are that one you know as Jesus, and we are happy to teach you today. We want you to know that for us, this is an act of love. It brings joy to our heart to share these teachings with you, to begin to open your minds to new ideas, to begin to explain what is going on in this world. You have been sold a bill of goods, and you have not been taught the truth. It has been somewhat frustrating for me not to be able to do this publicly, not to be able to do this in the light, so to speak. But now is a perfect storm! The church has lost its influence, and social media and the Internet have opened up a whole new world, so we are able to spread these truths freely, and you are able to read them and practice them freely.

Do not underestimate the strength of the egoic mind; it has been fed and nurtured and pampered in your society, and you are the victim of many, many untruths. So you are going to have to bring discipline to this practice. That is why we encourage you to begin the lessons of A Course in Miracles. That is the transformative process that you will need to go through to clarify your mind in a very timely manner.

There are many spiritual practices on this planet, and you are free to choose whatever you wish, but when you do the lessons of A Course in Miracles and come to understand the truth of reality, the truth of projection, and the truth of your perceptual misunderstandings, you will make leaps and bounds in the area of love.

CHAPTER 15

Add Love to Every Moment

SOMETIMES IN YOUR SOCIETY, YOU ARE GREATLY MISDIRECTED AND driven by long-standing programming, so you might be confused about what to do in some circumstances. What is the loving behavior? How do you know what the loving behavior is when you have been taught to behave in a way that is out of alignment not only with love but also with how you feel?

It is difficult to determine what loving behavior is because many of you believe you act in a loving way when, in fact, you do not act in a loving way. You are completely unloving in the form of your behavior or the words that you speak, but you believe you are right, so you are confused. If the ordinary parent is asked, "Are you loving?" he or she would say yes; however, he or she worries about his or her children. This is unloving behavior! Here is an example.

When you think about your child in some situation that is out of your control and you begin to worry, these are the energetic transmissions that actually happen: First, your belief that you need to control the situation demonstrates a lack of faith in love. It proves your belief in separation, and it makes you think that if you are not in charge, nobody is there to help. In this thought structure, you demonstrate your belief in separation from God and from any caring, benevolent force whatsoever.

So your first thought — that your child needs you to help control the situation — tells you that you are reinforcing your belief in separation, and when you worry about that child, you demonstrate a low frequency. You revel in fear and envision fearful situations for that child.

Let us say your children in elementary school have gone on a field trip to a museum or some such thing, and you envision them being kidnapped or left behind by the bus. You create powerful negative scenarios because you infuse your thoughts with fear, which is strong emotion, and you negatively use your creative, godlike abilities to hurt your child. Your child is the victim in the scenario you imagine, so you literally inflict hateful thoughts on him or her.

This demonstrates how confused you are in your society because you do not understand how thought works and how energy, especially focused energy, works. You know you are godlike in your ability to create. Focused energy is an energy that has a strong feeling associated with it, so when you feel fear, you literally enliven that thought with your focus and all that energy. Because you are godlike in your ability to create, when you entertain fearful ideas that viscerally affect the energy systems of your body, you can feel it in anxiety, in nervousness. You use your creative force negatively. This is how you manufacture scenarios in the world. You attract to creation and bring into manifestation fearful scenarios, such as war, disease, burglary, murder, rape, and shootings. That is the energy you bring into the world through the alignments in your mind.

Your Thoughts Create Your World

You have been taught that your mind and thoughts are separate from the world, but they are not. They are the generative force of life on your planet, and you have been indoctrinated in such a distorted way that you all manufacture the world you see out there. You are horrified at what you see, but that demonstration of what you call love, worrying about your child, is the frequency that brings the chaotic world into manifestation.

So in this particular circumstance, to love and care about your children is to act as if they too are held in the hands of God, that they too are guided by their own intuition, their own teachers and guides. You trust that because they are going on the trip, they are meant to experience whatever happens on the trip and will be fine. If you think about them on the trip and start to envision a negative scenario, be loving by short-circuiting that vision and seeing them in your mind's eye as having a good time, being safe with their friends and their teacher, and hopping on the bus at the end of the trip, satisfied and joyful. That is a loving act!

When we speak about situations as loving or needing love, a perfect example of how an ordinary human mind is out of alignment with love is when it is misguided into believing that worrying about someone demonstrates love for that person. No! Loving someone is thinking about that person as safe and happy and seeing him or her as enjoying life and his or her experiences, whether or not you are with that person. That is loving!

Consider your personal intimate relationships. When your partner is late arriving home, you might begin to envision him or her as having an affair or flirting with someone or being in a car accident. These are the lines along which your Western minds are trained. If you think this way, you will attract that very thing, frequency-wise, into your experience. It might not manifest exactly that event, but it will have the same frequency of the thoughts you hold with energy, passion, and emotion.

You know how it feels when you begin to worry. Your partner is meant to walk through the door at six o'clock and isn't there at six fifteen. He or she isn't there at six thirty, and you send messages with your phone and in whatever form you can, but you do not hear back. Your mind makes up negative stories, and you worry. You call this love. You say, "I love so-and-so. I wonder where he (or she) is. I hope he (or she) is safe," but your feeling is negative; the feeling is fear. When you say, "I hope he (or she) is safe," but you feel fear, the words are meaningless. It is the frequency you hold that is the creative force behind this universe! Your frequency is reflected back to you all the time.

We must redefine love here for you over and over again because you have been indoctrinated over and over again in the wrong way to love. In fact, you have been taught how to hate people or to envision them in accidents and to call it love. Do you not see how distorted this is? Do you not see how poisonous this is?

When you look at your own body and judge it and hate it and say it should be other than what it is, you attack the very thing that allows you to have all the joyful experiences, lessons, pleasures, and wonders of life. You attack the very thing that gives you those meaningful experiences and education. You do not love your body when you hate it the way it is and drag it to the gym and starve it and pound it into submission. That is not love, and you will find negative health consequences arising in the body. You will find twisted ankles and pulled muscles when you treat your body that way. You must look at your body with appreciation all the time, even though it is a symbol of separation and one of the most challenging aspects of this experience. When you bring loving appreciation to it as the vehicle you are temporarily driving and experiencing this world through, then you will raise your frequency and you will bring health, vitality, and sexual energy to the body. Those things tell you that you are thriving. Good feelings tell you that you are thriving!

When you bring shame to the body and accuse it of being sinful or dirty or unloving in some way, you are acting out of accord with love. For many of you, these distorted views have come through church teachings, such as that flesh or sexual energy is sinful or of the devil and will lead you into darkness. These are thoughts and ideas that make you feel bad, and because you are indoctrinated in them, they have a lot of energy behind them. You will feel a visceral reaction in your body when you shame yourself, when you shut that energy down.

Sexual energy is a creative, divine aspect of God mind. It is the vital creative force that is used in your life to bring into manifestation that which you wish. It can be in the form of children. Many beings love to have children and share their lives with them, and sexual energy is clearly used for that. Sexual energy is an enlivening and vital part of your creative self, and when you shut that energy down, you are unloving. One of the great tragedies in your society is that sexual energy is demonized and hated. It is considered shameful, so it is hidden and repressed in your bodies.

This energy, when it flows, brings creative, vital ideas into your imagination. When this energy flows, it allows you to dance and to feel pleasure in the world. When you close this energy down, you feel dead. You do not feel vital. This is one cause of aging. One of the great fears you have in your society is aging in an unloving way or feeling that you have lost your vital force. Well, that vital force is in the form of sexual energy. So when you have hateful ideas about this aspect of yourself or think it is wrong or distance yourself from it, you are acting in an unloving way.

Choose Loving Thoughts to Attract Love

These things are love: energy, vitality, caring, and kindness. Envision with love, and envision with creative, joyful ideas. Worry, repression, and self-hatred are all unloving ideas, and they will prevent you from bringing love into your life. What we want you to know is that the feeling of love you have for people does not come from them; it comes from you. Your feeling of love for someone is when you look on that person with forgiving, caring, and appreciative eyes.

When you look on people with judgment, you will not love them and you will think the problem is theirs, but you are the one who is being unloving. Judgment is unloving, and this is one of the great paradoxes of your society. You are taught that love is good, that love is something to strive for. You seek that special person, that special love relationship, but you are injected with judgment and with valuing the body as an object of desire. What we want you to look at pertaining to the body is what it can bring you in terms of experience. Where can it take you? How does it feel? This is the right use of the body — not as bait to catch somebody, but as a vehicle to express, transport, and experience.

So you see that your society is out of alignment with love in many ways, and you have narrowed it down to the pursuit of a special relationship because you lack love in so many areas of your experience. You lack love for yourself, you lack appreciation for your body, you judge the weather and other people, and you eat badly. Because you do these things, you lack love every minute of the day, so the special love relationship you seek becomes this god, this idol, that you must attain because you do not feel love at any time in your experience. You do not love yourself. You do not love your coworkers. You do not love the weather. You do not love!

You seek this relationship to solve all these problems, but it cannot solve the problems because when you lack love all through the day, you will not meet somebody of a high frequency because you do not hold a high frequency. You have been holding the frequency of judgment and attack with your thoughts about yourself and others. You have been holding the frequency of war when you disagree or argue with people all the time. So when you hold these low frequencies throughout the day and you attract someone to you (which you are perfectly capable of doing), you attract somebody of a like frequency: a judgmental, fearful, or attacking person. You will be innocent in doing this because you don't understand how unloving you have been. You attract an unloving person, and in a dysfunctional relationship, you seem innocent because you do not know what love is.

You have attempted to add love into your life by bringing people to you, but you have attracted judgmental, hateful, and perhaps even violent people, and you say they are the bad ones. You say, "Look, I am innocent. I am looking for love and doing everything I can to add love into my life." Look at your thoughts and feelings. If you feel lonely and isolated and depressed, you are in a low frequency and do not appreciate yourself, your fellow brothers and sisters, your life, or your body. You are not living in a way that brings love into your experience.

You cannot bring a loving relationship to you from that frequency. Your society has an abysmal record with love relationships because you are all unloving in the way you look at yourselves, each other, the world, and the weather. So many aspects of your perception are contaminated by hatred and fear and judgment that you are low-frequency people. Add drugs, alcohol, and violent television or movies to this, and you begin to see what a poisonous soup your minds are.

You must be comprehensively reeducated so that you can bring love into manifestation in your experiences. You must start with yourselves because you are the magnets, the frequency setters, the ones to attract others of like frequency.

If you are sad and lonely and depressed and are drinking and smoking and abusing yourself by watching violent television, guess who you will attract? A frequency match for you. You add pain onto pain, suffering onto suffering, and it won't be much fun because you will add another ego mind immersed in lack of love to your life, and that will double the problems. That is what all of you see in your love relationships: You add pain onto pain, suffering onto suffering, lack of love onto lack of love.

Honestly look at your unloving thoughts. How do you judge yourself? How do you judge others? How do you judge your workplace? How do you judge your families? If you think about these aspects of your life and you experience a dip in your feelings, then you know you lack love in these areas. If you think about an aspect of your life and you feel an increase in love — happiness, joy, or contentment — then you know you have love there. You can always add more love, but you know you are doing better in that area.

We do not want you to dwell on the negativities, but you must be realistic and accurate in interpreting your frequency. This is why we suggest you stop watching violent television. Doing so is a frequency-reducing activity. You watch death for entertainment, and the ego mind loves this. It feels good in the moment, but overall, you lower your frequency.

When you eat unhealthy foods, the ego loves this in the moment — the sweetness, the "deep-friedness," the fattiness — but overall, the body is attacked by unhealthy, "un-alive" foods. When you eat life-giving, fresh fruits, vegetables, grains, and seeds — foods that are still alive and will grow if you plant them — they bring more life into your experience. Look at your diet. Where are you unloving with your self? When are you eating dead foods? If they sit on the shelf for weeks on end unattended and do not rot, they are dead foods. We even hesitate to call them foods; they are food-like substances. Food thrives, grows, and lives, so it needs to live in your refrigerator if it needs to live with you for a few days.

We want you to understand where you lack love in your life. You will know by assessing how you feel. How do you feel when you think about your mother? How do you feel when you think about your children? How do you feel when you think about your partner? How do you feel when you think about your body? Each one of these subjects will either elevate or lower your feelings. If you feel depressed, go into that subject and look at the thoughts and ideas and beliefs that you hold around it. Practice forgiveness. How do you forgive those subjects? We go into that next. We are teachers of forgiveness and love, and that is why we are here with you now.

Your body can be your friend. Your family can be a source of joy for you. Love relationships can flourish and thrive, but you must understand what you do to sabotage them, what you do to attack them, and what you do to hurt yourself.

CHAPTER 16

A New Approach to Forgiveness

THERE ARE MANY OPPORTUNITIES FOR FORGIVENESS IN EVERYDAY LIFE, and there are also mistaken concepts about forgiveness. In your mind, forgiveness follows this process: Somebody commits a crime (or a sin or an act that you disapprove of), and at some point, you decide you will forgive that person. Usually, you either want to continue the relationship for some reason or realize that your upset is causing you a lot of distress, so you decide you must stop dwelling on it. You are trying to be a good person, so you step up to the plate. You plan to forgive the sin that has been committed.

This kind of thinking makes the sin or crime real; you perceive it as true. We use the words "sin" and "crime" synonymously because, generally speaking, when somebody steals a car or robs a bank, you think of this as a sin, something that is bad. Your definition of bad, your definition of a sin, implies that there are acts that should not take place. It implies there are things that this God you believe organizes your world cannot stop or prevent. So what you are actually doing when you say someone has committed a sin or an unforgivable crime is playing God. You are saying that God should not have allowed that to happen or was incapable of stopping it. You are, in fact, taking over the job of judgment that you believe should be God's. You are usurping God's will, in a way.

Consider the implications of this; they are massive. You are literally overruling God when you decide somebody has committed a sin or did something that should not have happened. From Spirit's point of view, everything that has happened should have happened. How do you know? Because it happened! It was supposed to happen because it happened. That is how you know what God's will is.

This completely destroys your view of the world — and rightly so. You are living in a world that is not created or ruled by God's rule. You are living in a world that is ruled by the ego. God's rules are ever loving while your rules are not. Stealing from someone is not loving. Killing someone for murdering somebody else is not loving. Beating a child is not loving, and walking past a hungry person on the street who has no money while you have lots of cash in your pocket is not loving. These are not the actions of a loving God; these are the actions of the ego mind.

The rules you live by are not God's rules at all; they are yours, the ego's. They are the rules of separation and judgment and fear and malice and death. Those are the rules you live by. Now, an underlying shift takes place when you begin to forgive. This is not the forgiveness we have just described here, the "usurping of God's will" forgiveness. We are talking about the forgiveness that allows everything to take place because it should take place. It is created by the beings involved, and they have the right, through free will, to create whatever experience they want to have.

The person who is burgled by the burglar has a frequency that attracts that action. The person who is murdered has a frequency that attracts murder. That is the creative process playing out on your planet at this time. Everybody receives the exact frequency experience he or she puts out so that it is perfectly balanced; it is perfect as it is. When you understand that separation and fear reap those frequency rewards, then you realize that nothing "wrong" is happening here. People experience the exact frequency reflection that they need to capture their attention.

This is how spiritual evolution begins: You begin to see patterns. You notice that in ten different scenarios, you get the same kind of response from different people in different places — from different employers, different landlords, or different lovers. You start to see that you are the common denominator to the negative things in your life, and in that realization, you wake up to the fact that you are bringing these things to you. Therefore, the person who hurt you is part of the waking-up process. The person who stole from you is part of your waking-up process. That is how it works. When you look at something and say that it should not have happened or that a person should be stopped and punished, you are, in fact, stepping into a natural balance of energies.

Of course, your society is built on many restrictions and rules of law that have nothing to do with natural laws, so you have become lost. People are deprived and separated from their natural selves, so you see aberrant behavior. To allow beings absolute freedom when they display aberrant, urbanized, crazy-making, insane, ego-driven behavior would not be a good step at this stage of the game, and it is not what we propose. We do not propose a sudden shift where everyone can do what he or she wants, violent or not.

Forgiveness Requires Acceptance

What I am saying is this: The restrictions and limitations and judgments and hatred and parenting techniques of your society are not working! They create aberrant and violent behavior and low-frequency reflections for many, many beings. We bring forth the seeds of change, information that you can use to shift your frequency.

Once again, when you watch television programs that show violence on the other side of the world or dark subject matter, you make that part of your world. If you turn the television off, those images and experiences and visions disappear from your mind, and you get to deal with your reality, with your frequency. When you turn that television on or go to that violent movie, you invite that negative frequency into your life. It becomes part of your experience. Turn off those importers of low-frequency ideas so that you do not deal with the added burden of fear and dread and death that those images put in your mind.

This will be your first forgiveness practice: Forgive yourself for being addicted to those things. You might feel fear and judgment and nervousness about stepping away from mainstream media and entertainment. You are going to have to forgive those things.

What I mean by forgiveness in this circumstance is absolute acceptance of the reality. If you watch violent television, you import low-frequency ideas. If you turn the television off, you eliminate low-frequency ideas from contaminating your mind. One of these actions brings you peace, and one brings you agitation and fear. If you choose the one that brings you peace, then you must stop thinking that it can do otherwise. What we mean is this: If you make a choice to listen to our teaching and you turn that television off, you might have thoughts and ideas that cause you agitation. You might think, "If I don't watch the news, I'll be uninformed." "If I don't watch the news, I won't be intelligent." "If I don't go to the movies, I'll be ostracized by my friends because they won't think I'm cool."

Such ideas might come to mind when you decide to stop doing these activities so that you can increase your frequency, and they can now become part of your forgiveness practice. In other words, you must allow them to surface, to come into your consciousness, and you must let them go. You must offer them up to Spirit to be taken from your mind. That is a forgiving act.

When you entertain and tell stories about those disturbing thoughts and ideas, you become agitated and believe them. Those are fearful practices. They are unforgiving ideas because they are not loving to you; instead, they attack you and cause anxiety. So our definition of forgiveness is about acceptance. If you make a decision to turn those things off, accept that decision, and do not entertain the unkind thoughts that might arise. If you make the decision to walk away from those things but do not come to a place of acceptance about it (you entertain those fearful ideas), then that is an unloving and unforgiving way of being. Forgiveness is about acceptance, peace, and love. An unforgiving idea is brutal and judgmental and anxiety inducing. A forgiving idea is loving, peaceful, accepting, and kind. You can bring these principles to any idea that arises in the mind, and that is where we want you to begin your focus. It is not about action.

As an example, let us say you resent your mother. You don't like to be around her because she upsets you or nags you or some such thing, so you choose to stay away from her to avoid the upset. But it is still in your mind whenever you think about her. You don't necessarily need to go hang out with her when you feel this resentment, but you can think loving and forgiving thoughts about her. Instead of focusing on the behavior you dislike — her judgments of you or her criticisms or her nagging — focus on positive things: She brought you into this world, she sends you birthday presents, she loves you, she nurtured you for many years as a small child, and she cares for you. Focus your mind on loving things, and when hateful thoughts come up, surrender them to Spirit. You ask us, in Spirit, to help clear those ugly thoughts from your mind. That is a forgiving act. When you entertain hateful ideas about her (think negatively about the things she says or does), you exhibit an unforgiving mind. It is unloving, and you create more and more dysfunction in that relationship by feeding those negative ideas.

If you dislike your job so much that you don't want to go there anymore and you feel your frequency decline when you think about it, bring forgiveness to your workplace. Tell a different story. You can say, "Well, that is where I work, so I must be there for a reason. I must have chosen it for a reason when I applied for that job. What was I thinking then? Oh, I remember — the job pays well and is conveniently located, and I thought it would be a good steppingstone in my career." We want you to think about the reasons you applied for the job. Nobody forced it on you. You said, "Yes, I will go there." You must take responsibility for your actions, and by bringing forgiveness to your thoughts, you begin to focus on why you chose that job.

Now, if you are still there and it no longer suits your agenda or your plans, then you must forgive it, for you have outgrown that job and must begin to focus on what you would like. It is not the job's fault that your shifting consciousness makes you want something bigger, perhaps something more stimulating or interesting for you. So you forgive the job you are in, you relax, and you begin to go to that job saying, "I chose this, and it's where I am right now. It's the job that I have right now." You can bring love to the situation.

How do you bring love to the situation? You bring forgiving eyes to your coworkers and the work you do. You begin to accept that you are there for now, and your stress levels go down, your frequency goes up, and you become happier. In your spare time, you can research some of the things you might like to do. Do you need to reeducate yourself? Do you need to relocate to have more opportunities? Do you need to make some phone calls to investigate other options? You can do this with a peaceful, accepting, and forgiving mind and heart. You do not have to do it when you are full of frustration and anger and judgment.

Everything Arises from Your State of Mind

When you approach looking at your options with a forgiving, loving, and openhearted consciousness, you will have a much higher frequency, so you will be much more likely to find a good position. If you come at it with an unforgiving mind and judgments, anger, and nasty stories going on inside your consciousness, you will have a low frequency, and guess what you are going to magnetize to yourself — a low-frequency job! You might simply slide sideways into another job you don't like. This is generally the way people deal with such problems; they bring a lot of judgment and hatred and negativity to a situation, and then they wonder why they attract the same thing. It's because they are blaming the situation and not their state of mind. Everything you experience arises from your state of mind. All your suffering arises from your judgments and lack of acceptance of what is.

When you accept what is, it does not mean you want that situation forever. It means you accept reality as it is, and in that place, you can make a sound decision. In that place, you can find peace because when you accept something, the resistance, judgment, hate, and low frequency stop. When you begin to accept it, your frequency, peace, quietness, productivity, and happiness all increase, and you are in a better position to make decisions.

This can happen with every situation you are in, but do not apply these principles to a violent situation in which somebody might harm you if you do not remove yourself from it. However, if you are in an abusive relationship and have been living with someone who has been hitting you or punishing you or hurting you in some way, accepting that you allowed this to transpire and that this is a reflection of your frequency is an important part of your journey away from that violence. When you can accept that mirroring is taking place, that someone cannot be hateful to you repeatedly unless you agree on some level (even energetically), then you will begin to understand your part in the creative process. No person is innocent of the creations he or she experiences. No person is innocent of the crimes perpetrated against him or her in a frequency sense.

This might upset a lot of you. A lot of you are going to say no. A rape victim is a victim, a murder victim is a victim, and an abused spouse is a victim, but that person would not be in that situation if a reflection were not happening. We are not saying the victim should stay, and we are not saying that the perpetrator should not be removed from society to prevent violence from happening again, but people who participate in such creative dances must, if they want to heal their minds, look at the frequency they have set for their lives. They are setting frequencies of victimization, and that is because of society's training.

How are you raised to be a victim? How are you raised to invite these kinds of things into your experience? We cover that next.

I am that one you know as Jesus, and I am happy to participate in these conversations. They bump up against your conditioning, against your societal rules, but they have to. We need to change your minds and your society, and the only way to do that is to bring truth into the light so that we can discuss it.

CHAPTER 17

Little Ones Need Freedom

THE JOB YOU HAVE IN YOUR WORLD IS A CONFUSING ONE. YOU HAVE BEEN taught to comply with many, many rules in your society, and you are taught this from a very young age. As we have mentioned before, victimization becomes deeply implanted in the mind. The victimized child is told to be quiet all the time, to sit still all the time, to keep his or her clothes clean all the time, to do as he or she is told all the time, and to behave and be nice all the time.

Little souls are very energetic when they first come into physical bodies; they come with a desire to live life. They create their physical bodies (you do not create those bodies for them) from their desire for life and their love of life and their impending explorations of experience that they envision for themselves before they even physically manifest on your world. But your society, with its ridiculous restrictions and hateful concepts, immediately begins to dampen these little souls' journeys into self-expression. That is what life is for! It is not to conform to others or to buy things or to get married; it is self-expression! You have separated yourself from Oneness so that you can be uniquely you.

There are positives and negatives to this. The idea of coming into separation is very traumatic for consciousness. It is difficult to be separated from All That Is. It is frightening to be separated from Oneness when that is all you have known, and that journey into separation is the same as birth, or that complete unity with the mother that the unborn child experiences. There are no decision-making processes, no worries about waste materials or food or even injury, but then you go on what can be a traumatic journey into physical reality, and that birthing process mirrors your consciousness.

Your consciousness wants to have an experience of individuality — singularity, if you will. It desires that, and so it happens, because that is your creative free will expressing itself. Then you realize with great shock what has been asked for, which is very much a case of "be careful what you ask for because you will get it." What makes the baby cry and causes the mind's suffering is this wrenching away from Oneness. But it is your choice, and you are prepared for it.

You have guides and teachers, and you have been given an impeccable guidance system that is strategically designed for your journey in life. In that little package of dynamic consciousness that wants to live is the desire to follow certain pathways and to experience certain things. You have even put things that you need to see in this lifetime in the family you were born into. You have put in those people issues and problems of your psyche that need to be resolved. This is why families are such a challenge for you. Because of the misteachings in your society and the repeated, long-term oppression and violent repression that you have designed in your system, the little beings coming in have a very difficult time with the restrictions and limitations of your urbanized, industrialized, repressive regime.

Lesson One: Be Quiet

In the West, you are told that you are free, but this is far from true. We itemize here some of the things that happen to you and cause you to become victims in your mentality, in your view of the world.

Your first experience is one of being told to be quiet. There are energies in a baby that need to be expressed, and sometimes the energies that cannot run, that cannot play, that cannot jump, and that cannot tell you that you are doing something it does not like have only one outlet, which is to cry, to show displeasure at what is happening through its voice. When you stick a soother in that baby's mouth every time it cries, you begin the process of victimization. You tell that baby that you don't care why it is crying.

Many babies in modern society want to be picked up. They are pushed around in strollers and shopping carts and lugged around in car seats, and they feel abandoned because they don't receive enough human touch. For those of you who have or will have new babies in your lives, we suggest you try picking them up before sticking a soother in their mouths. Pick them up, and soothe them that way.

By sticking soothers in their mouths, babies are given a victimized mentality that says, "When I am upset, I must be quiet." What happens in an abusive relationship in adulthood? One partner is hurt and is quiet. This behavior begins very early on, and the victimized mentality tells the person that she or he does not have a voice. The energy to speak up is not accessible because it was thwarted very early on in your child-rearing regimes.

If you have a new baby in your life, pick it up when it cries. Of course, there are food and diaper situations that need to be attended to as well, but your baby does not cry without reason. It cries for a reason, and it may very well need some flesh-on-flesh contact. That is a natural thing for a newborn to want.

Lesson Two: Be Still

Look at animals. They lie down with their babies and quietly nurse them. They are not in a busy world of productivity like you are in which household chores must be done, so they will lie down with their babies and nurse, nurture, and play with them. Your little ones need a great deal more of these activities. They are often shuffled from chair to chair and entertainment form to entertainment form rather than being picked up and cuddled and carried around.

This, of course, is exacerbated by the system that has been set up for the nuclear family. Often, the care taking parent is alone with the child. That parent might be responsible for maintaining the house, buying groceries, and doing all kinds of things that are very time-consuming. Then he or she has a little one to care for as well and might feel overwhelmed by the work and incredible loneliness. You live in isolation in your society. Your communal nature has been fractured and dismantled intentionally so that you are all raised to want your own home and to be alone, and this is how the little ones become neglected. One person cannot do all the work.

The natural situation for humans is to live in groups — communities — so that when a parent is busy doing something, a sister or an uncle or a brother or a mother is there to assist with the care of the children. Furthermore, in this situation, the children have their own family members to play with — cousins and brothers and sisters.

Isolation in your society creates a kind of victimhood because the parent who decides to provide the primary care for the child cannot cope with the loneliness and will often put the child into a sedative state with television, food, or a pacifier so that chores can be completed. So this is another place where you are hypnotized into doing things that you are not really in alignment with.

Imagine you are a two- or three-year-old child who wants to play, which is the natural way children learn (it is not a waste of time). Playing teaches you how to manipulate your body and your environment and how to interact with other beings. Let's say your parent or caregiver is there but busy — on an iPad or phone while he or she tries to get the dishes or laundry done and to clean up the house or cook dinner. These are all chores that would be done communally in a healthy environment but are being done alone, and so you, the little one, are plopped in front of a television because it pacifies you.

Once again, your system of direction, which tells you to run and play and pick up rocks and eat dirt and collect worms, is overridden by a society that does not encourage outside play and that values a tidy, big home more than anything else.

You continue on your journey into victimization. You are told, "No, you cannot run around and play. We want you to sit quietly and be a good little girl or boy. Don't make too much of a mess, because somebody has to clean up after you." This victimizing culture has the idea that this vibrant life force, this vibrant energy, is annoying somehow and needs to be quelled.

Of course, as you grow older, your parents know that you have to go to preschool or kindergarten, and they plan for this further restriction of your life force. They anticipate that their little rambunctious three-year-old, who wants to climb and jump and run, will be trouble in that classroom, so they increase their restrictions and their programming about sitting quietly. "You will not be able to run and jump like that at school, little Bobby, so you had better learn to stop that right now! It is not all fun and games once you get to school; you must do as you're told!" Do as you are told! That is victimization right there! This does so much damage to the little spirits that our hearts break to see the strictures and constraints forced on these little beings who come in with such joy and enthusiasm and who want to explore the world.

So this is where victimization begins, and it is a soup that you swim in, a soup that you bathe in, all the time in your society. The parents are not at fault; they are merely victims of the same system. We are not accusing the parents of being bad. What we are saying is that the system does not bring forth independent, strong, innovative, creative, spiritual beings. It brings forth repressed, controlled, victimized, and victimizing automatons that have no idea what their passions are or what their life forces are.

Lesson Three: Repress Sexual Energy

Another thing that happens is sexual energy is repressed from a very young age because children are told to cover up their nakedness. Why should little girls and boys have to cover up those parts of their bodies that are naturally beautiful, that are naturally self-expressive, on a beautiful sunny day? Very early on, parents chastise their children or push aside their little hands when they explore their own bodies and feel sexual pleasure. Children quickly learn that an angry face will confront them when they touch themselves in certain places. These are actions that repress vital life force. When you have a strong energy, such as sexual energy (which is a God-given, creative, vital energy connection to divine mind), being repressed or shamed or chastised for exploration at a very early age, then you enter very dangerous territory because that energy cannot be repressed. It will only go underground and pop up somewhere else in some other form because it is part of your life force. It is like trying to remove a leg: It is not going to be an easy task, and great problems arise when you try to cut off a vital part of your existence. Sexual energy is that!

Sexual energy is the creative life force you have been given to energize and motivate and express throughout your life — from the time you are little till the time you die. It is one of the great losses in your society, and it is an enormous amputation that takes place in your world.

Raise Children as Free Beings

Next, children head to school. Of course, we do not need to describe that process. We have gone over this before, but we want to remind you of the restrictions, judgments, evaluations, shaming, and so forth that take place. Seven- or eight-year-olds should not be stuck at a desk learning to read or write. They should be out gardening or building tree forts or climbing and running. Teaching can take place in those environments. The education you are obsessed with is not the right education for the world. It is the right education for the businesses and the economic system that your society insists you become a part of.

If you were raised as a free being, no one could force you to go to work for forty hours a week or insist that you do a job you hate. If you were raised as a being who honors the personal guidance system and trusts in intuition, you would not have a job you do not like, and you would not sacrifice your life on the altar of commerce. You would say, "To heck with it! I will find a piece of land somewhere, and I will grow some food and paint and raise animals and write music (or some such thing)!" The powers that be must make you so deadened that you will comply and allow them to victimize you.

This is where your victimization comes from, and this is the polarity you see in your world. You see, the victimizer and the victim have to work together; you cannot have only victims. You have the aggressors, those males who are trained in violence and aggression and strength and combat from the time they are little. Look at little boys fighting with their light sabers and their bows and arrows and their swords. They are indoctrinated in violence very early on. Look at those little girls who are told to keep their clothes clean and sit quietly and share and be nice and not argue.

There is a complete separation between the sexes' conditioning, and it is part and parcel of the rape culture you now exist in. It is part and parcel of the warring culture you now exist in. Many girls are trained to be passive and not to participate in politics and the ruling of society, and many men rule society by coming at it with warring minds and combative attitudes, happy to finance and use the war machine.

Your society's basic principles are set down in childhood through your families and your school systems and are ripe for change. They will have to change if you want to live in a world that is peaceful, loving, and kind and does not have victims and perpetrators. Boys must be allowed to be the kind, gentle, and self-expressive beings they are, and girls must be allowed to be the feisty tree climbers and self-expressive artists they want to be. We are merely giving examples here.

You need to be allowed to be who you are, and your parents need to honor that. You come in with specific desires and a specific set of goals, and you are ruled by your passions. When you are ruled by your passions, life becomes very good because the energies flow and there is constant guidance from Source. You can live a magnificent life.

You are likely a parent, a grandparent, an auntie, an uncle, a brother, or a sister, and you likely see someone in your life raise children. You are witnessing the perpetuation of the old paradigm rules, old restrictions and limitations, in this society in which you live, and we want this conversation to come out in the open.

How can you live with children and allow them freedom? How can you live with children and bring them up not only to respect themselves and their guidance systems but also to be kind and participate in communal life? These are challenging questions because you have such a deeply indoctrinated belief that good children look a certain way when in fact you are just raising victims and perpetrators.

This may be difficult to understand because you do not know how to change, but we are here to help you. You can make small shifts today in how you treat yourselves, your little ones, and each other. It must begin with you, and it must begin today. You have run out of time, so you cannot wait for somebody else to do it for you.

When that baby cries, don't stick a pacifier in its mouth. Pick it up, and give it some attention. Stroke its hair, put some cream on its skin, give it a massage, hang out with it on the bed, and talk to it. Tell it you are happy that it is on this planet with you and that you are going to do your best. When that little girl of yours gets her clothes dirty, just put some jeans and a shirt on her and tell her to go out and have some fun and not to worry about the clothes. It is much more important for her to have fun and to grow strong and adventurous. When that little boy wants a gun or a sword as a toy, take him to an art store, and ask him whether he'd like to get some paints and do some painting. These are the kinds of shifts you can make.

When you think about educating your children, don't think about school as it looks now. How can you educate them? What stimulating activities can you provide for them? What stimulating things can you show them about the world? Can you shift that system a little bit or even completely? Is there a progressive school that you can enroll them in? Can you home school them for a little while to give them more opportunity to live in a natural environment? Can you take them to the country? Can you allow them to explore nature more rather than the television and the computer?

You all have choices that you make every day that perpetuate the violence and victimization in your society. Do not sweep it under the rug or be unconscious about this anymore. You are running out of time, and your world will not survive if you continue with these regimes. It will not survive, and it is as simple as that!

I am that one you know as Jesus. It is time for you to step up as a creator. It is time for you to step up as a nurturer, as a stimulator, as an educator, and as a loving being to help those little ones around you live better lives. In twenty years, the world will not look the same as it does now, so training children to work at a desk is pointless. Such training will not provide them the skills and talents they need to live in the new world. Do not think that forcing them into that mold will benefit them; it does not. The world is shifting and changing very quickly, and you need a new generation of adventurers and creatives — of brave, loving, self-expressive, and self-nurturing souls — to bring this new paradigm into being.

That is our challenge for you: Look today at how you conform and how you cause your children to conform, and begin to break the rules a little bit with love and awareness. Know that you are bringing an exciting new generation into an exciting new world.

CHAPTER 18

Recognize True Love

THE SYSTEMS WE HAVE BEEN DISCUSSING ARE ALL PIVOTAL IN YOUR inability to love. We have been going over these systems because you must understand what is at play in your love relationships so that you can be clear about what undermines your ability to love not only yourself but also your beloved.

Your love for yourself must come first, and this is always what your Western-trained minds do not want to hear. Your love for your self must come first. Your love for your life must come first. Your love for your body, as the transportation and communication device that it is, must come first. Your love of your world must come first because it is in that moment-by-moment appreciation of all of those things that you raise your frequency into the realm of love.

What we are witnessing is a population of beings who are made by love, from love, and for love who are systematically removed from the experience of that reality. You do not believe those words — you are made by love, for love, and from love — because it does not feel that way. It does not feel that way because you are out of alignment with truth and you are not taught the truth.

When you read the story of my love affair with Mary [see *Jesus: My Autobiography*, Light Technology Publishing, 2015], you might feel jealous or envious or distressed that you are unable to bring forth that kind of love in your experience. But we want you to know that in that lifetime, my study was one of relinquishing hatred and discovering what love is. My incarnation was one of relinquishing judgment and embracing forgiveness as a demonstration of my understanding of the rules of creation, and in that study, I was rewarded with a complete alignment with truth. I was rewarded with that moment of ecstasy when my frequency went high enough that All That Is came streaming in and I had access to complete knowledge.

All I did in that lifetime was climb the ladder of love until I was in alignment with the frequency of All That Is, higher mind, God, if you will. Once you raise your frequency, love comes to you naturally because you are already in its frequency, and it can do nothing else. You struggle in your relationships on your planet because little boys are taught to kill and little girls are taught to hate themselves and judge their bodies and those of others, and you are kept deep in the materialistic, egoic consciousness that has been fed and nurtured on your planet for millennia.

Now, this is a very big job we are talking about. My excursion into love obviously generated a mythology that was usurped by the church structures of the time, but a great recovery period has been going on for several decades now. There has been a recovery from the repressive and brutal regime of the Roman Catholic Church, and slowly but surely, a reconnection with Spirit is taking place on your plane with a lot of effort on Spirit's part. This is not just coming from your side. It is coming with a lot of effort on our part as well.

Know What You Seek

You are now at that critical time when you have to make some decisions, and you have to really understand what it is that you seek. You seek the feeling of love in your life, and you have been told that it is going to come to you through another person. We are here to tell you that the other person will come as a result of you generating that feeling within you. Yes, from the ego's point of view, you can attract a partner, but that is what you see in divorces, brutal and violent marriages, and disillusionment. You can see the ego's world at play in relationships, and it is not a very fun one. Those of you who have been through a divorce or have experienced any kind of physical violence from your partner know that the ego's way is a very, very unpleasant experience.

Stop comparing the ego's journey to love; that is an impossible comparison. The ego does not know how to love. It only knows how to attack and judge and separate and be fearful. That is its nature. So we want you to stop comparing the love you think you know and begin to surrender to this practice that we bring. You must step away from the ego's thought system. It is a complete thought system, and we have mentioned this many times before. You cannot sculpt and value the body as bait and find true love. By doing so, you are immersing yourself in a low-frequency use of the body that will bring you a low-frequency experience of what you call love. Now, we do not use that word generously here. Most of what you experience is not love at all. After a short time, you will agree that the ego's games are very unpleasant and can be quite brutal and cruel.

We are speaking of real love. We are talking about getting your frequency into the realms of peace and happiness and joy so that you can attract real love, not just of the physical body. This is where your programming is detrimental to your search for relationships. You think that if you do not have access to someone's sex organs, you do not have love. That is not so. Any relationship that you choose to spend time in — a person, a good friend, and even art and music and nature (these are all love relationships) — should be given much more value on your scale of whether you have love in your life. You do not define these relationships as love relationships, but they are, in fact, that.

When you have an inclination to call a really good friend and hang out for the day, have dinner, or go camping, and it is not a sexual relationship but a close platonic relationship, that is love! Define it as such. Do not use qualifiers such as, "Oh, but we don't sleep together" or "We are both girls." None of that. We want you to say, "This is love in my life." If you write because you love to write or you sketch because you love to sketch, we want you to tell yourself, "This is love in my life." When you are drawn to something and you choose to participate in it, you are in a relationship with it, and it is fulfilling you. You are in alignment with love because you are feeling loving.

Creativity is one of the greatest connectors to the love frequency. If you love pottery or art or you feel great joy from listening to or making music — when you are in that frequency of ecstasy as you listen to a wonderful combination of notes or dance to that perfect rhythm — then you are in love with that thing! You join with it, commune with it, and you are in the frequency of love. The more you do things that you love or the more time you spend with those people, places, and things that you love, the more likely you are to find that special beloved of your own!

Love Is Created when the Heart Is Open

Mary did not come to me when I was sad and sulking and living a constrained life. Mary came to me when I was living a passionate life of following that which I was fascinated by and being immersed in the study of texts and principles that brought joy to my heart. Even when I disagreed with the studies in which I was immersed, I was passionate about my love for them. I loved walking in nature, having a good discussion, teaching people, and studying and learning. Mary came to me because I was always in love with my life, my journey, and my self-expression. She was drawn to me because of that, and I actually helped her to become more self-realized because, of course, she was a woman in a patriarchal, repressive culture, just as many of you are.

Now, you individually — both men and women — have freedom of choice. If you are aware, you are free to choose what it is that you want to do. Many of you say, "No, I am not free; I have a mortgage and a job." Do you know what? Those are your choices. It is true that you have been programmed to make those choices, but they are still your choices. You are not forced by anyone other than your own confused mind and inconsistent beliefs. You are coerced by your own thoughts into doing things you don't want to do.

You will see an enormous transformation on your planet over the next few years. You will see systems that you are a part of fail, and this is why it is imperative for you to begin this work voluntarily. It is imperative for you to redefine love so that you can enjoy the process of impending and approaching freedom because that is what will happen on your planet. You will go to work one day, and no job will be there for you. You will go to the bank one day, and the doors will be closed, and you had better have some awareness arising in your mind, some training in innovative thinking and forgiveness to be able to weather the storm that is coming to your planet.

We are not here to monger fear; the mass media is doing that job well. We are here to give you a heads up with love. Now is the time! You have been unconscious long enough. You all know the truths we speak as we speak them. You say to yourselves, "I know this. I know this. I know this!'" Well, you do *not* know this unless you practice it! You do not know this unless you feel it. You do not know this unless you teach it to your children. You do not know this unless you are living a life that is fully your choice and is fully in alignment with your desires and your values and your passions! Love is to live a life that is passionate, to know that you are doing the work that is *your* work, to know that you can get up every morning and say, "Yes, I am so happy to do what I have to do today, not because somebody is standing over me yelling at me or because I'm afraid that if I don't do it I'll be poor, but because I love how it makes me feel."

This is love, and it is the passionate love affair we want you to aim for, a passionate love affair with your life because, trust us, the beloved that is yours is there and has always been assigned to you, but he or she is at a higher frequency, not the lower frequency of fear and restraint and obligation and responsibility. True love — the kind you all seek, the kind you remember in the back of your minds — is a high-frequency love that is about mutual support as well as mutual recognition not only as equals but also of your spiritual, creative, and loving natures. You remember this because it is where you come from. You have been there before, and you have stepped down into separation and fear. You have become lost, led astray by the hierarchies of your society. We make no bones about this!

Take Responsibility, and Welcome Change

The hierarchies of your society have lied to you. They have manipulated you and taken you deep into dark woods. You've become lost, and you are afraid and don't know how to get out of there. We are here to tell you that you have a guidance system, a feeling inside of you that tells you when you are in alignment with what is right for you. When you hear the words of truth, there is a part of you that knows it's true. You must begin to act on those feelings. You must begin to say to yourself, "I will no longer work forty hours a week. It does not make me happy. I am going to go in, and I am going to tell my boss that I must cut my hours to thirty-five a week, and it is not negotiable."

You will be surprised. A lot of bosses will happily cut your hours a little because they are scarcity based and fear based and money based, and they will think, "Ah! We can get forty hours of work out of this person in thirty-five." Do your thirty-five hours; don't work harder to make up for what you would have done in forty because you will not getting paid for it.

Be brave. Begin to do these things. Turn your television off two hours before bed. Hide your children's violent video games. Suggest that a snowboarding or soccer game might be more fun than the first-person shooter game you have allowed them to play. Yes, *you* allowed them to play with it. You must take responsibility for the myriad unloving decisions you make in your life. When you make decision after decision that is unloving, limiting, and fear based, you do not feel love in your life. You do not look at your partner, if you have one, and feel inspired to make love or to cuddle and converse. Your frequency is too low to do that! You cannot do that! You cannot muster the energy to do it because you are too far down the emotional scale.

The same thing takes place in your relationships with your children. If your children annoy you by doing things you don't like, it is because love is lacking in that relationship. Perhaps they are locked in their rooms with their devices too much. Perhaps they never go out in the fresh air. Perhaps you are neglecting them because your frequency is too low. Love can always be added to every situation to increase the frequency. In this moment, you can make a choice to turn your television on and slouch around on your couch, or you can bundle up if it is cold outside or put a hat on if it is sunny and go for a walk and find a park bench or a beach or a patch of grass somewhere where you can commune with nature. You can take a journal and do some writing, or you can put some wonderful music on your headphones. You can choose to be more loving to yourself in this moment.

Do not deny love anymore. Instead, bring it into your life in every moment that you can, in every action that you can, and in every word and thought that you can! Bring love to you, and you will see it reflected in your world. As you raise your frequency, as you align with that which you love and with that which makes you feel better, you will see that love reflects out in the world in the form of the abundance, health, good relationships, opportunity, and new experiences that you want. The universe knows what you want, and it is ready to give it to you, but you must be in the realms of joy and love and happiness to receive those gifts. Those gifts are meant to bring you joy, but if you are depressed, the distance in frequency is too great. It cannot happen.

You must understand how this frequency elevation works. It is very simple. The better you feel, the higher up that scale you are; the worse you feel, the lower down that scale you are. Nothing is doing it to you. It is your thoughts and reactions and the stories you tell in your mind that cause every feeling you have, and that includes the love of your life. When she or he is not there and you feel lonely and sad, it is because of what you are doing. It is not because you are being punished, and it is not because that person does not exist. It is because your frequency is too low, and you cannot feel that person yet. That person is out there.

We go into the theory behind love relationships in the next chapter. Now we want to motivate you. Know that in this moment, you can do something to bring love closer to you, and you can do it very quickly by making yourself feel a little bit better.

CHAPTER 19

The Map to the Unaltered Soul

YOU ARE WELL AWARE OF THE REPETITIVE AND DEEPLY INDOCTRINATED desire for what we call the special relationship in your society. This special relationship isolates you from the world. This is the fundamental belief that you have to address. Focusing all your attention on one person who is not you is a profound act of separation, but you are told it is the opposite. You are told that it is communion and that the most important place to find love is in one special person, but because of the training in your society and the deeply judgmental psyches in which you live, this is a Catch-22. With the psychology that you are trained in, the psychology that is nurtured and strengthened in your society, it is impossible for you to find love because you are in too low a frequency. Not only does your society tell you to chase after the "one," but it also guarantees that you will never find that person because the other things it teaches you prevents it. In this Catch-22, no matter how much effort you put into finding love, the boundaries and requirements of the egoic consciousness in which you are immersed preclude you from reaching it because your frequency is too low.

You have been given a map that is inaccurate. You have been given a map that says, "Follow our dictates of the body, income, cars, education, leisure activities, and entertainment, and you will find the love of your life." Every time you go to one of those systems, you see pictures of happy people in love. You are being deeply manipulated by your society into doing the very things that stop you from experiencing the high-frequency feelings where love resides. The map your society gives you takes you into shark-infested waters, the waters of death and attack and destruction. All you have to do is look at your world to see that this is so.

In the West, you have some very limited views of what is actually happening on your planet, but you lose your power daily through these systems, and that is why Spirit is making such a concerted effort to intervene. You have lost your freedom. Those of you who have been deeply indoctrinated by the education system continue to be deeply indoctrinated by societal norms, and you have lost your ability to see clearly where you are going.

We are here to give you a map to love. It is not going to conform to your society's requirements of love, and that is going to be a challenge for you because you have been trained that it looks a certain way and that if you don't look a certain way, act a certain way, buy certain things, or live in a certain situation, you are not going to find love. But if you keep going on the track you are on, your society is literally not going to survive; it is not going to survive its lack of love. This map to an unaltered soul has come from deep within the nonphysical realms, and it tells you what you must aim for. It tells you where you must go, which is to the true part of you that is in alignment with love, the part of you that knows when it does not want to do something and when it does. To get to that part, you must remove the untrue part and be vigilant and disciplined. You will eventually become free. You are not free now. You think you are free to do what you want and chase after whatever dreams your society has told you are the dreams you should chase, but this is the truth of the matter: You have been deeply indoctrinated to chase the dreams of wealth and fame and big houses and fast cars, but these are all marketing devices for those industries.

Follow the map that is God given. It was given to you in collaboration with Spirit before you came to this planet very much like a map is given to an explorer. You must follow it to find the treasure, and that treasure is love! The treasure is your true self, free and self-expressive, and that is what you seek in your love relationships. You do not realize it, but you want to feel good and be happy. You want to wake up in the morning and feel excited about life, and you have been told that it is going to be by finding one person. You feel disillusioned until you find the right person, the one you think will save you from yourself.

I have good and bad news for you, dear ones. Nobody will save you from yourself. You are the creator, so everything you think about or want is going to come to you in the form of your experience, in the form of fractured relationships — your life. Until you understand the laws of creation and that you have been conditioned into intensely egoic thought structures, you will bring to you those low-frequency experiences in the form of death and illness and untenable relationships.

Unless you align with that map to your unaltered soul — the feeling self that you are in contact with every moment of every day — you will be lost in a desert, and you will see mirage after mirage. The love relationships your society tells you about and deeply indoctrinates you in are those mirages. You walk in the direction that they tell you to walk in, and on the horizon you see what you think you want just as that desperate person walking in the desert sees a mirage and walks faster and faster to reach it, but no matter how close the desired object seems, it remains an illusion. This is the "love" the ego tells you to follow: Be judgmental of yourself, work hard, and struggle. If there's no pain, there's no gain. These are some of the strictures and advice that the ego-mind gives you, but when you struggle, you are not in alignment with the map to your unaltered soul. When you suffer, you are not in alignment with the map to your unaltered soul. When you fight with your girlfriend or boyfriend, you are not in alignment with the map to your unaltered soul. Instead, you are in alignment with the ego's plan for consumption and war and death.

Create a Beautiful World

This world you live in can be a beautiful experience of individuality and self-expression, and that is what I ask you to walk toward. Walk toward your own self-expression not as it is dictated by your society but as it is dictated by that wonderful, ever-present map that you have in your heart, which is your feeling self.

You are exactly where you are supposed to be. As you read these words, understand that you have come to this place and have drawn this material to you for a reason. Now is the time! Your frequency, your plan, your map, has brought this experience to you, and now is the time for you to clarify your mind and get rid of the untruths that have been planted there. They have been planted there by marketing people, by the industrial war machine, and by governments that do not want you to stand up for your environment. These are where the messages have come from, and I ask you now to step aside from those messages so that you can save yourselves and open up to a world of love and to your own magnificence.

You have all been given the greatest gift in the world, and that is this: The human mind that connects to love can manifest anything it wants to manifest. That is what you learn in reading about my life on the Earth plane, and that is how I worked miracles. I was completely connected to love. There was nothing else in my mind, and I was able to transform the physical, material world. My crucifixion was a demonstration of that. Those beings on Earth who saw me live again after that crucifixion were destined to learn that lesson, but they did not all learn it because they had become so attached to my body.

As you come to the end of my part of this book, understand that I am not my body, and you are not your body. If you are waiting for that bearded Middle Eastern guy, that is not going to happen. Why? I overcame the body. I stepped into eternal life, and you can do that too! You can overcome the physical/material world through these spiritual practices.

You have everything within you in this moment. You have everything within you that you need to take this journey with us, and you have brought this message to you. You feel it! You are reading and understanding that the short-term, ego-driven goals of your society are destroying your environment, your happiness, and your fellow brothers' and sisters' home on this planet, yet it is all coming from within your minds, which have become disempowered and unconsciously violent and aggressive.

To end war on the planet, you must first end the war within your minds. To find love, you must love yourself and everything you encounter. To shift society's trajectory, you must shift your personal trajectory. If your idea of fun is going to a mall and spending money on things you don't need, you must realize that people who want to keep you small and immersed in the material world of the ego mind taught you this behavior. They do not have your best interests at heart.

Spirit and higher-consciousness beings have your best interests at heart, but we cannot override your free will or tell you what to do. All we can do is call you toward the truth and ask you to listen to how you feel. How do you feel when you are in alignment with yourself? How do you feel when you remove judgment from your mind? How do you feel when you are kind? How do you feel when you are cruel? How do you feel when you listen to that still, small voice inside you that wants to guide you on this most magnificent path to your unaltered soul? You can return there in one lifetime if you focus and dedicate yourself to the practice. It seems like a long journey that we are asking you to go on, but the truth is that life led by the ego will become worse and worse. You will get sick, age, and die, and it is not fun for those of you who are immersed in the suffering of the ego mind. It is unnecessary. You do not have to live that way. You can live a happy experience based on love and that still, small voice within you that tells you exactly where to go.

You might feel lost and overwhelmed with the life you have created for yourself. You truly have created it for yourself. Even if you have been following someone else's map, you have made the decisions to get mortgages or go into debt to purchase consumer goods. As you read this book, we are in alignment with you. Your frequency is tuning into our frequency; it has to. You are dipping into our realm, and we are not limited by bodies, time, space, or the other things that limit you. We know you are there! We know you need help, and we can help you, but you must ask. You must begin to do what we ask you to do so that you can examine the belief systems in your mind.

Take Steps That Make Sense

There is no point in doing anything now with the consciousness you hold. If you are unhappy with the things you have created and brought to yourself, do not throw the baby out with the bath water! Do not leave your marriage, job, or your children's homes, or do not sell your house. Simply begin to change your mind. Study this material, and listen to your guidance system, and as you go to sleep at night, ask us — Jesus, the Christ consciousness — for help. I am only a being who aligned with the Christ consciousness and woke up from the dream of the material world into the truth of your eternal spiritual nature. That is all that happened to me, and my many cohorts and I can help you do the same.

We are extremely high-frequency, high-consciousness beings who are here to bring you out of the darkness, out of the materialistic, body-focused ego world in which you have been indoctrinated and are imprisoned. You know you are imprisoned there because even though you don't want to do certain things, you still do them. There are two yous: There is the free you, the unaltered soul that came to this planet to experience uniqueness and its own special way, and then there is the you shackled with the ideas and teachings of your society that have imprisoned you in consumerism, like sheep led to the slaughter.

Yes, you are being led to the slaughter, and we are trying to stop the destruction of your society and environment. You will pull yourselves out of this. The more of you who pay attention to this teaching and follow this path to clarify the mind and open your heart to love in all its most magnificent forms, the better you will be able to stop and stem the tide of war and hatred on your planet.

This is not what you have been taught. You have been taught that it works this way, but look at how your system is working! Consider the fruits of the tree you have grown. The fruits of the tree of the Western way are environmental destruction, constant war, suicidal thoughts, and rampant consumerism all wrapped up in a very sophisticated package. That is the truth of your society and your life. You must now bring love to yourself and your world step by step as we instruct. There is a way out of your well-decorated and comfortable prison. You are all in prison, and we are here to help you free your minds. We are here to help free your hearts to teach you the truth.

I am that one you know as Jesus. I have come again through this particular form to bring you the truth without the body, and that is what you are. You are the truth, and you are not your body. You have a system that aligns with love naturally, and that is what you must get back to, but you need help, and I am here to help you. I am here to help you realize your natural, unique self, the unaltered soul that came onto this plane to bring forth this revolution. You are one of the revolutionaries who are preparing to change this planet into something unrecognizable. Together, we will change this planet into something unique and beautiful, a place of loving kindness in a golden era. It will be a wonderful, wonderful new world.

You are the creator, the free will ambassador of your own experience, and you must choose which god you are going to worship. Are you going to worship the god of materialism and the body, or are you going to worship the god of love, freedom, and self-expression? We know which one is the best. We have done it ourselves. We encourage you to follow love, to follow the truthful voice contained within your heart, and we ask you to do it now.

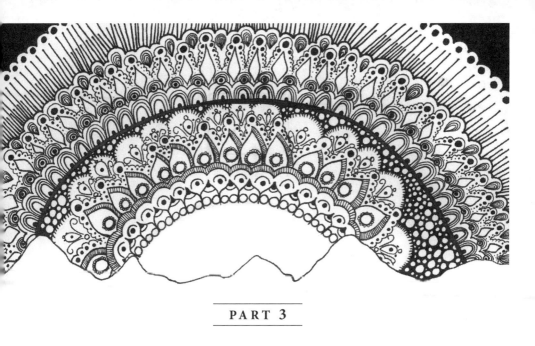

PART 3

The Love Story of Jesus and Mary
Ananda, Jesus, and Mary

CHAPTER 20

Strive for an Egalitarian Society

WE, ANANDA, ARE WITH YOU AGAIN, DEAR ONES. INDEED, WE HAVE A wonderful new development for you, and it is the arrival of a new being. It is Mary, Jesus's beloved partner. This is a surprise for you, obviously, although you might have had an inkling. She dictates a few chapters to add her side of the story to this wonderful library that is being generated by you.

So Jesus has a few words to say first. We want you to know that even though you are sitting quietly by yourself and there doesn't seem to be much going on, you are causing ripples around the globe at this point. Mary, of course, is the secret that is being revealed in these texts, and she has her own story to tell. Her love story is part of the revolution for this information to come through. We are very excited that you are participating in the revolution that has to take place in the minds and hearts of Westerners. They must look at their beliefs in God and their ideas of Jesus as described by the Roman Catholic Church, and they must open their hearts and minds to the fact that Jesus was married and had a beloved tantric partner known as Mary Magdalene. She will come through after Jesus says a few words.

A Loving Partnership Lasts Forever

The story that is about to be revealed is part of a revolution. It is only in transforming people's opinions about me (and consequently their opinions of Mary) that you will come into an egalitarian society. The fundamental structure of your society is patriarchal. It is built on lies about my life that were perpetrated to enhance the repression and control of half the population — women — by the men of the time. These are the foundational building blocks of your society, and you are still reaping that poisonous crop. That is why this journey into love is such an important one. Love is inclusive. Love does not divide, love does not demean, love does not hurt, and love does not rape. This is what we must look at together as we bring these truths into the light. We are not attacking men; on the contrary, we ask men to open their hearts and minds to the truth that they have been trained in a misogynistic and patriarchal society and they are inadvertently indoctrinated into abusing women by objectifying their bodies and seeing them as products.

You must view each other — men and women both — as partners, as equals, as fellow travelers on the same journey, holding hands and walking side by side. Only in that truth will your world be saved. As long as this patriarchy remains in power, you lose much energy, love, kindness, and joy because women are not respected or treated as the magnificent, independent, creative, spiritual, intelligent beings they are. The saddest part is that they do not treat themselves that way either because they are raised in a society that does not give them equal time and does not value them as independent, free-thinking beings.

We are not against anything. We are for love: love of men, love of women, love of everybody, love of life, love of nature, and love of animals. It is only by bringing these difficult ideas up that we can look at where inequality is.

Many of you in the Western world look around and think women have equal opportunity, and that is not so. From an energetic point of view, we see into the hearts and minds and physical structures of all of you, and we see where women are fearful. We see where women mitigate their ideas and inspirations, and we see where women attack themselves because they do not or cannot conform to society's rigid physical requirements of beauty and sexuality and these kinds of things.

How can we work together to change these things? Well, we must look at their foundations. That is what I am doing by bringing forth the story of my journey on the physical Earth plane.

My beloved has continued her journey at times with me and at times on her own special path. Even though we are in unity consciousness here, we all have special assignments, individual development assignments. The joy of living in a completely egalitarian and balanced and communal loving space is worth the work.

Begin the work of becoming stronger. For the women, this does not mean you should become more masculine. It means you should work toward being more divinely feminine. You are women, and you have natural tendencies to do certain things. Whether those are inventing a new energy system or growing flowers, it matters not. If your heart speaks to you of something, then you have the right to value that choice.

Men, you are not under attack. I was a man in a patriarchal society, and I witnessed and felt the pain of the women there. The pain of the women in your society is invisible. They suffer greatly because of the misogyny and patriarchy still in play, but their suffering is invisible because they are frightened of you and are uncomfortable in sharing their desires in this world because of the systematic and long-term patriarchal structures that exist.

Yes, there have been liberating experiences, but look at what women had to do to be given those experiences, such as the right to vote. They were not given that right; they fought for it. What we want you to do as the modern, liberated, awakening men you are is to actively help in this liberation program. Yes, it is a liberation program because it is in the West that the influence lies. It is in the West that the power and the money structures are at play, and as long as you participate in those patriarchal structures, you facilitate this repression.

I am not attacking anybody here. What I am inspiring you to do is to look around in your personal world and ask, "Where do I dismiss women? Where do I disrespect them? Where do I objectify them as bodies?" Begin the work quietly in your mind, which is where equality begins. It does not begin in action out in the world based on distorted thoughts and beliefs and ideas; it begins in a clarified heart and mind, where you look honestly at what you do to perpetuate these ancient systems. Yes, they are ancient — thousands of years in the making — and it is going to require all of you to do your work!

Come to this communication with an open mind and heart, and look at how it makes you feel. If something is said in this part of the book that frightens or upsets you, write that thought down. What and where does it come from? Did your church teach it to you? Did your family teach it to you? Do you not know who taught it to you? It is okay not to know where that thought comes from, but if it causes fear or judgment, know that it was put there by a system that does not align with truth.

Align with the truth and the understanding that love, equality, kindness, and forgiveness are the answers to the problems you have in your world. You are taught that war, limitation, and attack are the answers. That has been at play on this world for a very, very long time, and I want you to honestly look around and ask yourself how you think it is working so far. Join the revolution of love! Go inside and clean out those closets full of old skeletons, old beliefs, that aren't yours anymore. They might belong to your parents, your church, or a culture you no longer align with. You must remove them from your mind to see clearly. These beliefs are lenses that cloud your ability to see the truth and stop you from finding love. Anything that is out of alignment with love will interfere with your ability to manifest love in your world.

Now, this woman, when she was physically manifested in a body on the world (just as I was), was my great beloved. She still is. Although we do not have physical sexual relationships in this level of consciousness, we are bonded through that experience and through a profound eternal love. This must be brought into the light of your confused culture so that you can understand more deeply what kind of person I was and what my life looked like. As long as you believe I was a celibate, patriarchal participant, you will act that out in your world because you see it as sanctioned and perfectly permissible. It is not. That is not who I was or what my life looked like, and now is the time to hear an aspect of that story that you have not heard in this form before.

There are many, many beings channeling at this time, and each brings forth a different aspect of the story based on alignment and frequency, so sometimes you hear variations on a theme. We want you to know that the purpose of all of these communications is to open the mind and heart to love, equality, and mutual respect.

Know that we are with you as you read this material. Reading it brings you into the frequency in which we reside, and if you accept this teaching as something you want to align your frequency with, then you may begin communications with us. Understand that the book *A Course in Miracles* is the path to the clarification of mind that is required for truthful communications, and you must go through an initial clarifying and cleansing process to begin. There are so many lenses distorting your perceptions, and you must go through this process not because you are less valuable but because you *are* valuable.

You must understand what has been done to your minds in your Western society, yet it is very difficult because you live in the mind that has had many, many programs inserted into it, and we ask you to be willing to relinquish some of your false self so that you can be more aligned with your true self. Your true self is a magnificent, eternal, spiritual being who has no fears and only knows its love, its truth, its joy, its passion, and its purpose.

In studying the lessons of *A Course in Miracles*, you will not lose anything that is valuable. Instead, you will allow those thoughts and ideas that bring negativity, fear, and confusion into your life to drop away. We know it is a great act of faith to step into a mind-training program that is unknown to you, but you have been immersed in mind training for your entire life, and now is the time to take your mind back.

Now is the time to stand firm in your belief in love and in your knowledge that when you feel bad, something is wrong and when you feel good, something is right. If anything said makes you feel bad, look at why. Do not just drop the book and say, "This book makes me feel bad." This book brings untrue ideas to the surface of your emotional guidance system. It is like a filtration system that brings the dirt and contamination to the light so that you can have a look at it. You cannot deal with something if you do not know it is there. So as we journey into this part of the book, be brave, pay attention to how you feel, and write down any of the negative feelings that come up. They will be the beginning of your new practice of clarification.

We pass you over to Mary: my beloved, my equal, and the most amazing partner I could have wished for on my journey. We are no longer bonded in the same way because it is not required. Freedom, self-expression, and creativity are honored here in all ways, and we each have a path to follow; however, love lasts forever. Love always lasts forever. Anybody you have loved in your life will be with you forever. You will not be separated by death because there is no such thing. It is an illusory aspect of your limited consciousness, and it is one of the things that will transform as we evolve together out of the darkness that you have been contained in for so long. I am Jesus, and I say with great honor and respect, here is my beloved Mary.

CHAPTER 21

Connect Within

I BRING FORTH THE TRUTH OF MY RELATIONSHIP WITH THE ONE YOU know as Jesus. As we go into this part of the story, understand that what I tell you here is very different from what you have come to understand about not only him but also the fact that we had an intimate partnership that is not recounted in your histories.

You know that at that time, there were no newspaper reporters accurately recording what was going on because they did not know what was going on. The stories and the legend and the mythology were created subsequent to the event. Imagine hearing a story about something that happened twenty years ago and writing about it as if you were there when you were not. How accurate can that be?

You are faced with this in your society. You have been fed stories about somebody by people who were not there and who wrote hundreds of years later about something with which they were not even remotely involved. Keep this in mind as you read these words. This story does not conform to the mythology that most of you believe because it is pervasive. From childhood, you have been told these stories. So if you feel (which you likely will) disrupted or disappointed or disbelieving, realize that you are reacting normally, given the indoctrination that your society has inflicted on you. You have been told lies as if they are truth, so the truth will seem a lie. You must remember this. You have been lied to and deeply indoctrinated for reasons that will be revealed over the next few years. The story you understand about me is completely untrue. My journey with my beloved has been nothing but joyful, and now is the time for the truth of our relationship to be brought into the light so that you can understand us and what my experience was. My life with that beloved man was a most challenging and difficult and beautiful incarnation.

I have had many incarnations since then; it was not my last one. Even though I became enlightened, aspects of me continued to gather information through different timelines, and some of you have encountered me from those different timelines. As we go into this part of this love story, it is very important for you to understand that there is more than one timeline.

There are many probable realities, many probable pasts and futures. There are many dimensions in which different aspects of each of us experience different things. You have been told that reincarnation is a long line of historical incarnations that lead to this moment. That is not so. You have a multifaceted, multidimensional, multi-timeline experience taking place, but because your consciousness is limited at this time, you only take in a very small amount of information. That is all you can handle. Relax into knowing that a lot more is going on in your greater mind, your higher self, than you are aware of, and much of that information is coming through your emotional guidance system, or your feeling self.

During my physical relationship with my beloved, many things occurred in that time and place that limited me as a woman as well as us as a couple, so this is how I want to begin our story. I want to tell you my life story as it related to Jesus. We went through our personal and our shared journeys, and that is the story we bring to you now. Here, I talk about my relationship with my beloved. I speak about my experience of his life so that you can understand what love looks like, how it feels, and who I was. I was Jesus's beloved Mary. He loved me with all his heart and soul, and we were and remain deeply connected.

A Relationship without Fear

I met Jesus when I was a teenage girl. We were both part of a ragtag group of young beings who would meet beyond the oppressive eyes of our families and teachers and spend time walking in the fields, mountains, and hills of our homeland. Jesus was a powerful young man. Of course, he was very beautiful to me because he was my beloved, but even so, he was a very handsome young buck. I use this phrase because that is what he was, full of confidence and life. He was also full of wisdom, and that drew me to him. We became fast friends.

The religious restrictions that oppressed women fascinated me, and they became a topic of great discussion between us. Jesus's love for humanity and his profound connection to Spirit, which became clear early on in our relationship, guided him to treat me as his equal and cocreator on our journey. That is how he looked at me. He looked at me as somebody in his life who created experiences with him. This is very important for men and women both. Instead of seeing each other as combatants in a battle for supremacy, see each other as cocreators of a collective experience. What you give to the other, you receive. The respect that you give the other, you receive. The love you give the other, you receive. When you bring this perceptual filter into your love relationships, then there are no battles, no threats.

The battles and threats that occur in intimate relationships are the ego's attempts to have supremacy and control and to reduce fear. This was not part of my relationship with Jesus, because he was in direct conscious contact with higher realms. Higher consciousness guided him. He had some cultural teachings that we bumped up against once in a while, but because he brought forth teachings from higher realms, he did not heed them.

You will go through that journey yourself. You will go through the journey of reprogramming yourself into alignment with love as you go through these books. You will bump up against thoughts and beliefs and ideas in your mind that do not agree with love, yet they feel as if they are part of you. You feel as if they belong to you somehow, but that's only because you have taken possession of them for such a long time.

Jesus traversed those beliefs that bumped up against love, and we worked them out together. We had an unusual relationship. We were a young man and woman, but we were friends, and that was something that was very difficult to achieve in that time and place. We both stepped away, to some degree, from the religious and cultural restrictions of the time. When we ventured into nature or hung out in the orchards or by the lakes and rivers and seas of our local environment, we were away from those limitations, and we were in communion and communication with the truer parts of ourselves.

Retreating from society is an important thing for you to do as well. As you learn to reprogram your mind by stepping toward love and away from the separation and violence of the society in which you live, you will need to step away from the mass. That might be the mass media, the mass at church, or the mass of humanity. You will need to step away from those groups that are influenced by the hierarchies and histories of your world. You will need to step into nature with or without a beloved friend.

Early on in our relationship, we took ourselves away from the structures that were oppressive, from the structures and the eyes of the systems that influenced us at that time, and we became grounded in nature. This is a wonderful practice for those of you who are opening to love. Visit nature. Feel the sun on your skin, sit on the earth — perhaps garden or plant seeds — and get in touch with the more natural rhythms of your planet. You see, the structures you live in now are artificial, as is the information you receive from your mass systems. The natural environment is where you connect more to a true experience of your authentic self. As you step away from the cultural traditions that place requirements on clothing or appearance or status, you will calm down and be able to have more access to spiritual truth as it arises in your guidance system.

Jesus and I experienced that. We would sit in the shade of a beautiful tree, propping our backs against its trunk, and we would ground ourselves in the natural environment and speak honestly and from the heart about how we felt about oppression and control. They were not so different then from what they are now. The systems that were in play then are in play now. They have different names and agendas in some cases, but they are principally the same controlling systems that do not want you to connect with the truth of who you really are. I fell in love with Jesus as we sat under those trees or on rocks and gazed out at the beautiful landscape where we lived. It is heartbreaking to see what is happening in that part of the world now, and one of our great motivations is to relieve some of the suffering on your planet.

Love is eternal. Love is timeless. It is not of the body; it is of the heart and mind and spirit. Do not be deceived by bodies. They are temporary coverings for the truth of who you are, your heart and your mind. Your ability to love and to discern are your greatest skills, and as I tell my story, as I shift from this nonphysical realm through this channel to bring forth this experience that I had in my physical incarnation, do not think that that incarnation is more important than your incarnation. I was a spiritual being housed in a physical body for a certain time. You are the same. We are all equal, we are all valuable, and we are all coming to understand the same truth: The body is temporary. It is a low-frequency place in which you reside for a little while. It is not your permanent home. Your permanent home is in love, in eternity, and with all of us.

I am Mary Magdalene, the lover and wife to the man you know as Jesus. He was infused with love to such a degree that he took me on an unforgettable journey that deserves to be told.

CHAPTER 22

The Sting of Separation

AS I SPENT TIME WITH JESUS, NOT ONLY DID HE BECOME VERY DEAR to me as a friend but we also experienced that special connection that develops between a man and a woman. Now, this next part of my story is going to be very hard for many of you to believe because you have these ideas about society in those days that are out of accord with the way it was. Young men and women then were no different from young men and women you see now. We were interested in each other as physical beings, and Jesus and I spent a lot of time together with and without our friends. We became so familiar with each other that any boundaries seemed ridiculous. When we became lovers, the structures of our society seemed irrelevant, just as they do to young people now.

You see, my family was broken. My mother was quite poor, and she fell on hard times because of her history. We won't go into that — there is no need to tell story after story — but the truth is that I was left to my own devices a little bit. She had difficulties and was shunned a little from society. I was shunned a little too, and this is where the original story of my questionable reputation came from. That is where it was plucked from, but it was embellished and embroidered and made into something that never was.

Even though I was Jesus's lover and we were not married, this was not an unusual pastime for teenagers then. The parents of that time and place would deny it — the parents of that time and place did not see it — but as in your time, young beings found ways to sneak off together and have some fun.

Now, our relationship was one of love. It was not a superficial, frivolous, or tawdry relationship in that sense. Its very foundation was spiritual in nature. Jesus was already teaching in his teens, and he was the leader of that ragtag group of rebels. He received downloads of truthful teachings from higher realms from a very young age, twelve or thirteen years old. By the time we became lovers, he was deeply immersed in these teachings and lived a very spiritual life based on them. Those teachings, which were about being openhearted, feeling emotions, loving each other, and understanding that the body and sexual energy are not sinful but sacred, really guided our relationship. If those principles were used in that frequency and were honored and respected, then there would be no need to suppress or repress or stop teaching them. We practiced the principles of the teachings he received from his nonphysical teachers.

Following the Heart's Desire

You can see that your story about those times is distorted. Your history has come through the filter of a church system that has a specific agenda and story it wants to uphold. That was not our story. Our story is the truthful relationship of a young man and a young woman who were fortunate to be a little outside of the systems of constraint and repression.

Jesus bucked the trend of early marriage, which was a tradition we were all supposed to join in and follow. Because of the disreputable nature of my family, I was not considered good wife material, and as bad as that was for my mother (she lamented this and felt bad about it), in a lot of ways, I was very happy about it. It gave me more freedom than the more reputable young women had. Those young women were married off very early to conservative and controlling men who were deeply immersed in the religious structures of the time. I was given two very precious gifts: freedom and the love of a beautiful, spiritual man who had a higher value system than the limited and judgmental structures and limiting beliefs of the time. Being shunned by the structures of the day was a great gift.

We worked and studied together to learn that material. He was my teacher in those years. We meditated and wrote out the teachings together. In fact, Jesus helped me learn to be a very good scribe, which was not something gifted to girls then, and it was another great boon I received by not conforming.

We traveled far and wide working on this material together. It upset some people when they saw an unsupervised girl out with some men, and that is where the stories that I was a bad woman came from. That was how I was viewed. I was not viewed as a freedom-seeking spiritual student of a beloved master. I was seen as a reckless and poorly behaved teenager who did not care for the rules of society, and on that, those judging me were right. I did not care for the rules of society. I cared for the love and teaching I received from this most magnificent prophet who I was blessed to be in love with and who was in love with me.

I lived at home with my mother, and we often had the group of beings that we hung out with over for dinner. Jesus would regale us with tales and imitations. He was a very good mimic. He would make us laugh heartily with his impersonations of the stiff and rigid rulers of our small communities.

He was a teacher. That was his passion, and that is what most of our conversations were about. He brought through a great deal of information that was not in alignment with the religious teachings of the time.

I was his partner, and everybody knew it. This was not a dirty little secret we kept hidden. It was accepted and understood. I had had many conversations with him about this when I became concerned that we were not married. He told me he was unable to marry young because of the path he was on and the things he had to do — the journeys both inward and outward that he would have to take.

I did not understand what he meant by that, but as time passed, it became clear that he was going on a long trip, and I was not welcome. Because I adored him, when he told me he was going on that long trek, I became furious with him and was unable to contain it. I even threw a couple of girlish punches at his chest and yelled at him, begging him to take me with him and not to do this to me because I did not know how to live without him.

The Power of Fear and Heartbreak

I was terrified that he would never come back. I was terrified that if left alone, I would be married off to somebody or oppressed in some way.

I thought that because I was a young woman unprotected by a man, I would not have any recourse but to bow down to oppressive rules and regulations. This was as terrifying to me as the thought of losing him to another woman while he was on the journey. Of course, that is what every young woman might imagine would happen with a handsome, charming, and awakened young man on a trek by himself. My mind was full of frightening scenarios, and they brought my rage to the surface. It was an intense fear of losing him to the world, a world I could not see and was not welcome in. I really did not understand his point of view, and when he left on his journey, I would not talk to him. I was so enraged and fearful that I stayed in my room and refused to kiss him and say goodbye.

Of course, this was one of my great regrets in life, but it was how I felt at the time. I was full of passion for life and for him, and I was angry at the decision he made to leave me, to abandon me to the dangers of society. It was a dangerous society for women. We were bullied and enslaved, and once again it was my family's lack of standing that helped me keep my freedom during that time. If I had been an upstanding and socially acceptable young woman — wife material — I would not have made it through those years without him there.

But I made it through those years. As painful as it was, I made it through, and next I will go into some of my experiences during that time so you have an idea of where I was emotionally, spiritually, and romantically. I loved him dearly, and I could not think of anything worse than not seeing him for several years. It broke my heart, and it took me quite a long time to even come out of my room and attend to the daily household chores.

CHAPTER 23

Finding Personal Peace

YOU MUST REMEMBER THAT YOU ARE LISTENING TO THIS STORY WITH your own thoughts and ideas about how things looked back then. You have a story about Jesus, a story about me, and stories about the structure of our society and the priorities and habits of people you really do not know anything about. It is important to put those thoughts aside and recognize that you have been indoctrinated in certain things. Society is society, and there is no great difference between the feelings and emotions and behaviors of people in my time and people in yours.

What happens to a young woman now whose boyfriend goes away to university or joins the navy or army? After spending so much time with him and falling madly in love with him, often at a very pivotal time in her life, suddenly that rug is pulled out from underneath her. Her parents see she is living in her room for weeks on end, and they desperately worry, wishing she would get back to life and telling her that there are lots of fish in the sea (among other such phrases that parents hurl at their heartbroken youngsters). Of course, when you fall in love for the first time, your heart does not have any restraint or defenses. It does not have any wounds or dark spots, so it feels more strongly than any other heart on the planet. It is a shame that those who have been injured and divorced and disillusioned dismiss this profound and intense separation anxiety as childish or immature when, in fact, it is a very truthful experience of separation.

Remember, separation is the nature of this place. Throughout your lives, you experience it until you come to a place of reunification of mind. That was part of my journey of self-understanding, the intense love and appreciation I'd heaped on Jesus when I was in his presence. Remember, I was conditioned in a patriarchal society, and in my mind, he was a lot more valuable than I was. I thought his needs were a lot more important than my own. I was deeply indoctrinated in that program, and when he left, all those things came into my conscious awareness.

I was a student of Spirit just as you are. You are reading these types of books and learning that when you suffer profoundly, you are doing something wrong. You are out of alignment with love. We learned the same teachings back then that you are learning now. This is common between us. Our lives are not different, yours and mine. We have all been indoctrinated in society's values. People empower those values and believe them and act as if they are the truth, and then as they evolve, they come to see that some of those beliefs must be untrue because they cause such suffering. They learn that suffering is not necessary and is an illusory, self-induced state that is a profound separation from love. That was the teaching I had, and that realization began to surface as I lay curled up in a little ball on my meager bed and cursed Jesus.

I was angry and hurt and frightened and alone. I felt very alone. My mother tried to coax me out of the room, and I would have none of it for some time. The suffering was excruciating. As I began to calm down a little bit, I realized that the situation was what it was: He had gone. He had left me, and I would have to deal with my feelings and thoughts. I would have to live in that mind of mine and that body of mine and that world of mine. Jesus was no longer there to run interference for me. He was no longer there first thing in the morning to grasp my hand and walk with me out into the wonderful natural environment to talk and to love each other. My home felt bleak and empty. I realized I needed to put into practice some of the lessons we had studied.

Practice Being Present in the Moment

We are brought into this world with our own structures — our family, our society, and all those things that reflect qualities in us — and we come to a certain point in our lives when those limiting ideas and beliefs begin to cause us too much difficulty, so we begin to awaken. If we are fortunate enough to be in the presence of truth, we are given the material we need. Of course, I was blessed with the most magnificent deliverer of truth that anyone could have, and that was in the form of the young, vibrant, and youthful Jesus.

Do not doubt my gratitude for my experience. I am one of the luckiest people to have manifested on this physical plane to have had that experience with him, but as you know, it was not a simple life; it was difficult. It brought into my experience all my fears, worries, and judgments about myself, other people, and even him. This was one of the darkest times of my life because I did not know whether he would come back, and I was living in the home of a single mother. My mother was alone, taking in work (laundry and sewing, these kinds of things), and she was not welcome as an upstanding woman in society, so neither was I.

As the time passed and I began to help her do the work, I found solace in keeping busy and in practicing what I had learned in those years as a spiritual student with Jesus as we made those wonderful journeys into nature. We would sit by a river or lie on the wonderful foliage and discuss the thoughts and suffering that the disconnected mind produces. We talked about relationships based on fear rather than love, and we talked about love being free, truthful, honest, and authentic. As I surfaced from my deep anger and resentment of him and began to bring forgiveness to my mind and to my relationship with him, I saw that I had a choice. I had a choice to believe in the worst, which I could tell was not in alignment with truth because it made me feel bad, or to remain present and to trust that life would bring me the experiences that I would need in order to develop my consciousness evolution. I realized that was what we had talked about time and time again and that I had not been abandoned with an untrained mind. Rather, I had a very sophisticated spiritual education for somebody so young.

I had been exposed to truth and love day after day after day. I knew that if I was in pain, then I was not in alignment with truth or love, so I immersed myself in helping my mother with her business, and that and the knowledge I possessed were my salvation. On the outside, I looked like a single young woman who was very quiet and dedicated to assisting her mother's efforts to provide for the home. On the inside, I was a devoted spiritual practitioner, and I focused on love to the best of my ability.

Use Times of Trial to Practice Love and Discipline

Trust me, in the years when Jesus was away, I had some very difficult days, and my mother was upset with him for the pain it caused me. On days when my mood was good enough, I tried to explain to her that my thoughts, fears, and judgments caused my pain, and nothing was happening other than untrue ideas in my mind that were creating images of his infidelity or me being alone for the rest of my life.

There was another experience going on, and that was of a single, unprotected woman who did not have a good reputation because of the ridiculous standards women were judged by at that time. I was very careful when I walked along the street. I kept my head down, and I did not challenge anybody. Crude comments were often made about me and my relationship with Jesus, and the other young men in our group seemed to take a darker turn as well, stepping away from me. Without Jesus there to run interference, their relationship with me became complicated and caused difficulty for them and their families. As long as I was with Jesus and clearly his primary relationship, then the other boys were not questioned, but once I became single again, the ease with which we had spent so many hours together conversing and learning and teaching dissipated. Not only did I lose the companionship of my beloved, but I also lost the companionship of some of my other friends. It was a very difficult time.

As I look back on my journey through that experience — and of course, in hindsight, we see things that at the time we did not understand — I see that I had to develop some strength and discipline. When you are in the company of a great teacher, it is very easy to allow that person to take the lead and to let that voice rule your world. It is very easy to follow the teacher's stories and instructions, and of course, as a conditioned young woman in that society, that also contributed to my taking second place, so to speak. But during the time when Jesus was away, I had to develop some backbone. I had to become fearless and stronger, and I had to practice the teachings I had been taught for quite some time by that point. I had to put them into practice in my mind and in my life, and there was a lot of material.

I had a lot of forgiveness practice to do with Jesus, with the friends who would not hang out with me, and with my mother, for she was very short tempered with me when I fell into a depressed period because I could no longer discipline my mind and stop the thoughts and ideas that wanted to be generated there. She would become frustrated with me, and I had to listen to her nag me and tell me that there were other young men, that I could find somebody to marry me, that it was time, and that I had to let Jesus go. He was not good for me, she would say. Clearly he did not love me. This barrage was very difficult for me to handle. I had a lot of forgiveness work to do with my mother, and because I was living with her and working closely with her, it became very tense.

I learned in my practice that when I brought love to a situation, it always worked out better. When I thought about Jesus's return or the great joys that we had had together or the positive future we would have, my mood improved and my optimism grew. When I imagined him sleeping with somebody else, marrying someone else in a faraway place and never coming home, or being assaulted by bandits, these images caused sadness and deep suffering. I saw clearly and unequivocally that whatever I thought about generated my feelings, and what generated my feelings generated extreme emotions and upsets at times. It even led to big arguments with my family because my thoughts generated fear.

As you travel through your life, there are times when circumstances arrange themselves so that you have to practice the principles. It is one thing to practice those principles when everything is going well and you can sit quietly in a climate-controlled room. But when you lose your job or your partner walks out on you or you are sick or you injure yourself in some way, those are the times to put those practices into action. This was really what was generated in that experience for me. I was so well versed with the principles and had talked about them and come to understand them deeply in my studies with Jesus that when I actually had to implement them, I had a great resource to call on. When nothing bad is happening and you practice your forgiveness lessons and study spiritual material, it seems as if it might be unnecessary. You could just forget all this, and everything would be fine. However, this is a world of separation and fear, and you must prepare yourselves for experiences generated from your consciousness that, in your separated state, look like they happen because of a crazy world and have nothing to do with you. As you become more evolved in your consciousness, you comprehend the truth: The thoughts, beliefs, and ideas you hold to be true generate the circumstances in your life.

Like Frequency

As I suffered the slings and arrows of accusations, jeering, and nasty comments, I realized that these comments and hateful thoughts and ideas were coming from a disrespectful place in me. Where was I not respecting myself? Where was I attacking myself? Where was I less than loving? Every time I felt those attacks from the outside, I turned it around and asked myself, "Where am I doing something of like frequency? Where am I doing something like that in my own mind?" And sure enough, I could very quickly identify that, yes, I was attacking Jesus for following his inner guidance. What was I doing in breaking the rules of my society? I had to trust in my inner guidance. How could I attack him for doing what I was doing too?

In such realizations, you can begin to practice compassion and forgiveness on a profound level. When you begin to turn situations around and ask yourself, "What am I doing that is of like frequency?" you begin to see that we are all the same. We all come from a place of confusion. Some of us have great wisdom contained within our consciousnesses, yet we also have great untruth, and that is what we seek to remove from our minds. That was what I realized when Jesus was gone.

We had no telephones or any way of communicating with each other beyond the history we had together. I knew he loved me, I knew he was an upstanding and honest young man, and I knew he intended to come back. I had to cast my fate to the wind. I had to cast my fate into the destiny I believed we had together. I was rewarded on many levels with dreams and intuitions and feelings that he would return.

I had conscious contact to a certain level at that age with my guides and teachers, and I received information in the form of dreams sometimes. I could see myself married to him and spending time with him at an older age, and I knew that these were messages from Spirit to help me maintain my equilibrium, my hope, and my patience. Of course, young people are not patient; they are dramatic. This was a time to be tempered, a time to grow, a time to strengthen my resolve and will, and a time to focus on inner discipline. My feelings were generated by what I focused on, and I had a choice in every moment of every day whether I would be helpful and productive and assist my mother in her difficult life or sulk and fantasize about disastrous scenarios that would cause me to cry and become upset. Clearly, I was the creator of my own suffering. I knew the teachings well enough to discern this early on in the process, and that helped me through the whole thing.

By the end of my time without Jesus, I had grown tremendously. I had become a very serious practitioner of my own kind of spiritual discipline. I no longer relied on him; I had gone inside, and I was doing it for myself. This was a powerful gift. At the time, I believed I was practicing these disciplines so that I would not suffer. I was practicing them so that I would not generate hateful ideas, and I was doing the best that I could in very difficult circumstances.

I survived, grew, and learned, and that is the lesson I ask you to take from this chapter. When you face difficult times, take these teachings to heart, and use that time as a stimulus for discipline. Use that broken leg or that divorce as a stimulus for transforming your inner world, knowing that these seemingly random outside events are not random or outside you at all. They are generated from within your consciousness, and if they are not any fun, use that lesson and that time wisely to transform your inner terrain so that you do not need to have those kinds of experiences again. They tell you that there are some low-frequency ideas in the mind, and you can take that to heart and discipline yourself to learn, to grow, to be more loving, and to be more forgiving.

CHAPTER 24

Love Is Inclusive

MY TIME APART FROM JESUS DREW TO A CLOSE, BUT I WASN'T AWARE of that. The entire time he was gone, he was completely gone. I did not know whether he would be gone for two years or four years or eight years or twenty years. I was determined, however, to wait for him. You must understand that he was not replaceable. Some of you have had great loves and have chosen to remain single after that great love because you could not envision feeling that way for anybody else. That was the case with me. It was my decision, and the same goes for those of you who have chosen not to pursue another love. It is always possible to pursue another love, and despite my actions in that time and place, I would like to address this subject because it is important.

The mind that believes there is only one love in life is a mind that is delusional. So yes, my mind was delusional at that time. I claim an exception because of whom I was dealing with, but the truth is that once the mind has decided that only one person will do, then everybody else disappears from the planet. The mind is closed, and a closed mind is unloving. In my own way, I demonstrated my lack of understanding of love. I had shut myself into a limited person and into a limited space, and I waited, waited, and waited. Now, because of my relationship with Jesus and the kind of experience we were destined to have together, there is a little difference. He told me to wait, and I believed him. Because I knew

169

who he was and his spiritual nature and practice, I knew he would come back. I believed with all my heart and soul that he would come back. Still, I shut down during that period. I was not an open or happy person. I closed my heart to the entire world, and that is the issue I want to share.

When you love only one person (even when that person is present with you) and he or she becomes your idol who you worship above all others, then you are essentially in an unloving place. Because you have dismissed the rest of the world, you have dismissed the rest of the beings you meet as less-than that person; they are less valuable, less worthy of your time. If you have this idealized image of another person, you will see that you are less loving, generally speaking.

One of Jesus's great teachings was to love everybody the same. This seems impossible for most of us. Early on in my life in that incarnation, it seemed so to me, but the teaching is true. We can bring love to every interaction we have. We can bring love to every holy encounter we have because that is exactly what every meeting is. Every meeting is a holy encounter with another divine aspect of God mind, and we should bring that kind of attention to it.

The state of being that I was in, however, was not as a highly evolved soul. I was a young woman, and I was doing the best I could in a bad situation. I was struggling, there's no doubt about it! I had good days, and I had bad days. One day, as I was outside hanging up some washing, I looked up to see the figure of my beloved walking along the road toward me. I had been a diligent student. I had been such a hard-working spiritual practitioner that I had kept my heart open to him. If I had not had those teachings, I would have married somebody else; I would have gone into fear and thought I needed somebody else. But those teachings took me on a journey into Mary — into my own mind and into some very dark places. Fear of the future is a very dark place, but because I had been a good student and became a very good practitioner, I was openhearted as that figure walked toward me.

I recognized his walk, the sway of his arms, and the way he held his head, and I ran to his arms, just like in that romantic scene so often portrayed in movies. That was one of the most amazing moments of my life not only because my beloved had returned to me but also because I was openhearted and wasn't angry or resentful. I had done the work of love, and I reaped the rewards of it.

As you journey into your mind, understand that when you keep your heart open, align yourself with love, and put resentment aside, you will reap the rewards of love and attract to you — or perhaps, as in my case, back to you — that which you seek as a love connection or communion with another being. Now, these relationships are not always sexual. Sometimes the love practice returns you to a parental relationship, such as to an estranged parent or child. If you practice forgiveness, you will open your heart, and that is a powerful generator of reality as you experience it. Thought brings things into manifestation. If you have a relationship that is fractured or is over as far as your ego is concerned, do the forgiveness work. If there is a possibility for reunification or communion, it will happen when you are in the frequency of love.

I will not go into the few hours after my reunion with Jesus. Those of you who have been madly and passionately in love know what happened. We could not get enough of each other. We were all over each other. Jesus had transformed into a powerful man. He had known what that journey would do for him. He had known that to stay in this small place with the people who had known him all his life was one experience, but he needed to travel and grow and learn and explore not only the physical world but also his relationship to it, and he had honored me by not marrying me sooner. It did not seem so at the time when he left, but once we reunited, I saw that the expansion he had gone through was a gift to me as well. The expansion and the knowledge and the wisdom he came back with were his wedding gifts to me. He became such an amazing teacher, a well of information and wisdom, that my life changed forever.

It is very difficult in the fearful, egoic mind to appreciate the potential in what seems like a difficult situation, but once you apply love's principles, which are forgiveness and staying present and keeping out of the future fearful scenarios that the egoic consciousness wants to elaborate on, you can acquire benefits and rewards beyond your limited ideas and understandings at this time.

As we joined together once again, there was a profound interaction and an energetic shift in our relationship. Jesus had learned many techniques of meditation, prayer, and dimensional travel on his explorations of mind. His channeled teachings had continued and strengthened, and his ability to commune with nonphysical beings, teachers, and frequencies had grown tremendously. We practiced together daily, sharing those experiences, tantric practices, meditation practices, and conversations, and these practices powerfully contributed to the bond we experienced.

We fell in love all over again, and our sexual relationship transformed into one of great power. There were experiences of ecstasy and bliss and communion not only with each other but also with higher realms that took place as part of a developing and enlivened relationship that is difficult to put into words. It must be experienced to be understood. These practices were not picked up and the results not achieved with a few weeks' worth of practice. At that point, Jesus and I had been together for many years. He had been in communion with Spirit directly for almost two decades, and I had been an intensely devoted spiritual student.

Transformation Takes Practice

These experiences did not fall on inexperienced shoulders, and as enticing as these stories are, you must begin where you are. You must understand that these were the experiences of very devoted practitioners who do not live in your time and place. This is very important for you to understand as you wish for these things.

You have very low-frequency experiences going on in your Western world from your chemically infused and processed food, your violent culture, and your mass media. Many things are going on that stop you from reaching these heights. As you read this book, you might feel some sadness because you cannot imagine living the way we lived. It is very challenging to shift your consciousness and, consequently, your behavior into alignment with these kinds of things.

Know that every moment you spend in nature is valuable in your spiritual practice. Every moment you do not watch television is valuable in your spiritual practice. Every moment you take to read wisdom texts is valuable in your spiritual practice. Do not dismiss it. Understand that a quiet day spent in contemplation, prayer, exploration of nature, and study might seem as if it's a wasted day from the ego's point of view, but from our point of view, you raise your frequency so significantly that you transform yourself tremendously. We can commune with you so much more easily when you spend a day like that.

Do not restrict this practice to the weekend. If you have a job, take your practice there with you. Meditate as you do tedious tasks you do not enjoy. Recite mantras to help you, and use your forgiveness practice with your coworkers. If you do not want to be there, bring love to the situation just as I did when I was alone with my mother, struggling through those years. I realized I could suffer intensely and deeply by lamenting the situation, or I could envision the future I wanted. I could open my heart and send love to Jesus (even though I didn't know where he was), and you can do those things too. When you are at work doing a mundane task, use a mantra or say that loving prayer. Envision yourself doing the work you would like to do, whatever that is. You will know. Your guidance system will tell you. Your passions will tell you.

Being Positive Creates Influence

The next two to three years with Jesus were the best! We got married. He succumbed to tradition because it was time. I wanted to have a child, and I had done my part in allowing him his explorations, so he did his part in honoring what I wanted, which was to be his wife. Although I wouldn't be honored in society (because that was something that would not be given to me), I was honored by him and his friends and cohorts on this spiritual journey.

We did not know what was coming our way, but we knew we were having an intensely spiritual experience together. He began to get inklings that something was coming. He was warned that great change was coming in his life, and I was very nervous at times when he told me these things because I did not know what our life would look like. Nevertheless, for some time, we were as normal as we could be. We had not been normal before that. We had broken some rules and had behaved out of accord with tradition, but at that point, we conformed. However, we were old for getting married in that time and place, and there were certainly some raised eyebrows and whispers about that.

We had become far more than an ordinary man and woman. We were a sacred and blessed couple, and that was a great part of our relationship. We functioned in the normal way on the outside. Jesus did his teaching and some work to earn money. We lived in a small home, and I did the usual things that women did at that time — prepared food, cooked, gardened, and attended social activities — but in our private lives, we were intensely spiritual and always worked toward raising our frequency, communing with Spirit, and connecting with each other. Consequently, that was the most delightful time I ever experienced. I have had many incarnations, and in the timeless place in which I now find myself, I remember all of those incarnations, but that period after Jesus's return — our reunification as lovers and spiritual teachers — was the best time of all my lives.

This story is not designed to torment you into wishing for something you cannot have. It is designed to inspire you to raise your frequency into the realm of love. It is designed to encourage you to bring to your experience a loving divine relationship, and that, of course, must first be with yourself.

The time that I was alone showed me where I was out of alignment with truth, and it forced me to discipline my mind. You, as modern Westerners, have minds that are very distorted by indoctrinations and programs, and your work is cut out for you. Everybody incarnated on the physical plane has the same work to do, and that is to choose love in every moment you can. Eliminate hateful thoughts about yourself, and catch yourself when you judge others for their appearance or behavior. Remember that you are the creator of your experience here, and your frequency sets the tone for your future experiences.

You are no different from anyone else. You are no worse and no better. You are only limited by your ability to focus the mind, and the only thing of importance at this time is focusing the mind on love and on what you want to have. Focus the mind on what you appreciate and on what is good, and don't look at what is not right. One of the great misteachings of your society is to look at what is wrong all the time. You constantly lower your frequency because you have been taught that looking at the suffering of others is compassionate. It is not!

When you look at the suffering of others and believe in it and fear for those who experience it and hate or lament the situation, you literally lower your frequency and do not help the situation. When you look at a beautiful garden you planted, appreciate your friends and family, and eat well and look at yourself with loving and forgiving eyes, you raise your frequency and bring more and more influence.

Jesus and my pursuit of love together, our collaborative journey, brought more and more influence, and that was what created the ministry and Jesus's experience of enlightenment. It created the transformative teachings that changed the lives and minds of so many. If we had not been focused on love, those experiences would not have come to us.

Jesus's destiny is one he created by his relentless pursuit of love, and because I was his beloved, his partner, I went on that pursuit of love with him. Although we shared many experiences, we did not experience the same life. His life was very different from mine. Mine was that of a woman of the time. I was left behind sometimes, and I looked after the children more than he did, but it was a completely egalitarian relationship. He never valued me any less because we have different experiences. He valued me as he valued himself, and that was his contribution to the frequency of love. His love for me was unending, and he showed me great respect and compassion throughout the years we spent together. That period before his enlightenment, as I said, was one of the greatest times for both of us. He loved that time too. It was an easy time, a quiet time, a very loving time between us. Our experiences, both physical and spiritual, were beyond words.

I want you to know that you are not different from me. I was carried along on a tidal wave of energy that was associated with that beautiful man, yet I had my own work to do. I had to discipline my mind, learn to value myself, and delete beliefs and ideas I had been taught that were wrong. It was and is hard work. That is why we are here, helping you on your daily practice to love yourself, to honor yourself, and to train your minds to focus on the good, the kind, and the forgiving.

CHAPTER 25

Protect Love

MANY ASPECTS OF MY LIFE HAVE NOT BEEN COVERED IN YOUR HISTORY. You have been given a limited, one-dimensional view. We must look at why this is so.

At that time, there were no paparazzi or newspapers. Local gossip was the way news spread. I have told you about the reputation I had as a rule-breaking young woman and the freedoms that gave me. This is important for you to understand as we go into the next aspect of my experience as Jesus's wife and partner because there was only word of mouth that brought forth any stories about me. As you know, the gossip mill loves negative stories much more than positive ones. We began our journey into the ministry you recognize as Jesus's, and it was inaccurately documented in various forms over the years. We kept many personal aspects of our life private. As you see in your celebrity culture, it is very difficult to do that. Nevertheless, we made a concerted effort in that area, as it became clear that something very unusual was going on.

We became pregnant shortly after our wedding and went through that joyful experience of having our first child. Jesus, as you know without question, was a magnificent husband and father, caring and kind and compassionate. He spent a lot of time with our first child. Those were the best days, and we continued to devotedly pursue our spiritual practices together. Jesus's channeling information was very, very strong, and it was not something he could walk away from. He never walked away from it. It was a big part of our partnership, pleasure, joy, and delight.

You must remember that we lived in an oppressive, regimented society. The country in which we lived was occupied, and there was a lot of dissent and control and judgment. The teachings that were coming through to us were counter to that. They were revolutionary in the sense that they were based on love, forgiveness, and peace.

Shortly after Jesus returned and resumed his teachings (yes, he was doing informal teachings in our home), it became clear (from their fearful reactions) that the students did not want those in power to know they were studying this material. There was a great deal of fear.

Jesus and I decided, as our children came into the picture and concern arose about the safety of what we were doing collectively, that Jesus would take that teaching to other places rather than keep it around our particular small town. Now, this began before his enlightenment. He was a dedicated teacher and practitioner of spiritual principles and instruction. As I fell into that role of mother and focused on the home, it became clear that he needed to take his show on the road, so to speak. There were times when he was gone for a few days with his compatriots to teach and take these wonderful instructions from Spirit to others.

I was fine with that. I was happy with my role as wife and mother. I was what you call a domestic goddess. Because of the nature of my practice, I removed all judgment from the role I played in Jesus's life. I was completely content, and his love and honor for me allowed me to fulfill those domestic roles without any kind of rancor or judgment. Of course, it was the accepted role of women at that time to do that anyway. We did not have the issues of equality playing out then as they are in your society now. It is important for you to know that in Jesus's eyes, this was not less than the work that he was doing. I practiced the same spiritual principles in terms of understanding, but he had a direct line to Spirit that I was not blessed with. I accepted that. I knew he had his own path to take, and I had mine. We worked together as a completely balanced team in terms of agreeing on things. His traveling was part of that agreement.

Part of that decision was based on the fact that his teachings were revolutionary and somewhat inflammatory. He preached about independence, love, and forgiveness. He did not reinforce the teachings of the time and place in which we lived, and that was a dangerous act to bring out in public. We felt that it was much safer all around for him to take these teachings on the road and to begin this ministry away from home so that there were no inflammatory or confronting issues there. He wanted to keep the children and me safe, and he also wanted to have a quiet place to come home to where his revolutionary ways would not follow him. So we chose to keep our relationship and our children and our marriage out of the picture, so to speak.

This perpetuated the idea that he was single and childless. He did not broadcast or bring his personal life into his teachings, and he asked his fellow travelers to do the same. This agreement was made for safety purposes because of the nature of the material taught. As Jesus's life played out in public, it became more and more difficult and dangerous, and in fact, as time went by, we became even more committed to the idea of keeping the children and me out of what he was doing. He knew he was playing a very dangerous game. He was informed of this from Spirit. Not divulging his family life gave him the freedom to go on excursions away from his hometown and have privacy and space when he returned.

Give What You Want to Receive

When Jesus came home, nobody in town knew what he had been up to or what he had been teaching. It was not broadcast on social media like everything is in your society. When he came back from whatever journey he had been on, he was the local guy the residents had always known, and our presentation looked quite normal. That changed over time as he became more and more well known, but in those years, that is how it was, and it was of great benefit to the peace we wanted in our home and marriage.

Was I jealous of his going off on the road by himself? No, I was not. Our spiritual and tantric practices and our sexual and love relationship were powerful, bonded, and sacred. There was no jealousy on my part. I knew beyond a shadow of a doubt that this partnership was holy to Jesus, and he treated it as such. Our relationship was based on our spiritual practice together, our understanding of the same material, and our cooperative dedication to work out any issues we had through conversation and prayer and meditation. These were all employed to bring a healthy balance and a loving and sacred quality to our relationship.

To add a sacred quality to your own relationships, make it your priority to align with love — but not in the superficial, distorted definition you have in your society. This book brings forth all of the ideas that limit and restrict you, and you must come to know yourself. Journey into the interior worlds of your mind and your heart to really understand what love is and what it feels like and how to achieve it. Love is achieved within your mind and through your focus, your priorities, and your care. Love is gained through all those practices; it does not arise miraculously from nowhere. It comes from the vibration and focus that you hold, the forgiveness you practice, and the understanding you have that this world reflects your frequency. You bring to you that which you give. You receive that which you give. It is a completely reciprocal world.

In my partnership with Jesus, I gave what I wanted to receive, which was unconditional love and acceptance. I was not there to limit him; I was not there to judge or control him in any way. I was there to support and love and honor him. It was not a one-way street. He honored and loved and respected me and my choices and my desires as well. Our relationship was egalitarian in all ways, even though it might seem traditional and patriarchal to a modern Western person looking in from the outside. It was not. He completely honored and loved me and my ways and my preferences, and he had no value judgments about any kind of behavior.

Obviously, Jesus could align with love in a way that was exceptional and unique, and that precipitated his enlightenment. That is a whole story in itself, because in that time and place, he caused me some consternation, and our relationship was challenged a little bit by the massive shifts in his consciousness and then, consequently, in our relationship. But in that period before his enlightenment, our relationship was solidly forming and was, by the time his enlightenment transpired, blessed with two beautiful children.

CHAPTER 26

Love and Enlightenment

WE WERE LIVING A WONDERFUL LIFE, AND THE INCIDENT THAT LED UP to Jesus's enlightenment was not within my realm of experience. One day, he left to take care of his daily business (I did not know what that was, as I did not micromanage him, as you call it, in any way). There was no unusual feeling or any kind of expectation for a momentous event; he simply did not come home. Anyone who loves his or her partner will understand how distressing that was for me.

The time he normally came home passed. All I heard was that something had happened, that he had disappeared from the group he was with. We did not have a psychic connection to such a profound degree that I was able to understand or receive information that he was okay. Of course, as the mind plummets into fear and enters the realms of worry and panic, frequency dips and any communications from Spirit are very, very difficult to receive.

Here is something I recommend to any of you in a relationship with a person who is behaving out of accord with his or her normal routine: Don't go into terror. Stay calm, and see if you can pick up some information from Spirit about what's happening with that person. I did not know that. I had not been through anything like it before, and Jesus and I had not been separated for several years at this point. We had been living a close, intimate, and happy life together. Weeks went by, and my concern grew.

The beings he went on that day trip with had assured me that he had not been hurt; in fact, they reported that something miraculous seemed to have transpired. He had seemed to be inundated with some great energy and had wandered off, telling people to leave him, so they did. They said they finished their day's work and expected to meet up with him, but he was nowhere to be found.

What was unusual about this whole thing was that we did not send a search party out for him. We did not assume the worst, even though I was extremely worried and angry with him at times. Something in me knew this was not a completely negative experience.

I chose to focus on my training and my mental discipline, and I knew that once it was time, he would return. However, I will make no bones about the fact that I did not feel peaceful for the entire time he was missing, and as anyone could guess, I fluctuated between praying for his well-being and wishing that he would never return. I also fluctuated between intense longing for him and anger with him for not giving me a message of some kind.

You must remember, news was all word of mouth. I had received all the information I would get from those beings who had been with him. Obviously, something drastic happened, some spiritual event that was bewildering for those who witnessed it, and it had motivated my beloved to walk off into the woods by himself. I spent a very stressful month looking after the children and trusting (if not knowing) that he was okay. I believed in my heart that if he had been killed or injured, I would have known. That was female intuition, and I trusted it and kept myself together as best I could.

A Welcome Return

Several weeks passed, and it was not clear to any of us where Jesus had gone. Finally, he sent a message from his mother's house, where he had gone initially to recover from the traumatic and ecstatic event that was his enlightenment. The news that he had not come straight home and had gone to his mother's house instead made me even more furious, but in our subsequent conversations, he explained his motivation and why he had done that. At the time, I saw it as a betrayal, and it caused me great suffering, but through my spiritual practice and my understanding of the principles of creation, I was able to bring my mind into a semblance of sanity and peace.

The last week was almost more difficult than the first few weeks because I knew he had emerged from the wilderness and had gone to his mother's home, presumably for repair and respite. That was the message I received. It was not until he walked in the door of our house that I was able to let go of the tight grip of control I had placed on my emotions. I fell apart; there were no two ways about that. I cried and was angry and relieved, all those things that you would be if your beloved had been missing for several weeks and had gone on some mysterious excursion into heaven knows what!

I had gone through all the crazy ideas the ego explores: infidelity, insanity, crime — everything. I had done that, but of course, knowing Jesus as I did, these flights of fantasy were not that long-lived. All in all, I'd had a terrible time, and I was exhausted. When he walked through the door and opened his arms to embrace me, I was angry and confused, but he was alive, and that was all I cared about. It was all that mattered to me. I went to him and allowed myself to be embraced in the second most glorious hug of my life.

We sat down together. We held each other, and he told me what had happened to him. As the story unfolded and he revealed the most miraculous event, my calm returned and my awe expanded. I knew and he knew what had happened. As he told me what he was able to do, experience, and witness in the energy systems and matrix of reality, we knew not only that this was the end of his ordinary consciousness but also that it was what our studies had led us to as a couple and him to as an individual. As his partner, I was inextricably involved.

As he told the tale, he said that he needed me more than ever, that this would be a very challenging transition for him. He was struggling greatly with the battle between his ego consciousness and the new level of consciousness that he had been blessed with. It was going to require our collaboration and my unconditional love and support to get him through it. Of course, after those weeks of separation, I was more than happy to offer my compliance and absolute agreement.

Over the next few days, he physically recovered. He had been quite depleted by this influx of energy. He had stopped eating and had become quite thin. His week at his mother's house had mitigated this somewhat, but he was still not himself, and he spent a lot of time alone and ate little. I kept trying to feed him wholesome, fresh, and nutritious foods, and he tried to eat, but he kept telling me that food was not necessary for him anymore; he needed to eat very little because the energies he accessed through this amazing journey into higher levels of consciousness were feeding him. He had to cut back drastically on the amount of food he ate. He said he just did not need or want it. He only ate the bits he did, I think, to keep me happy and to give me something to do, because I was going through my own process.

I knew I had to learn to understand what his experience was because I was not having it myself, so it was difficult for me when he told me that he could see into the very heart and soul of each being that he communicated with. He could see where sicknesses and unhealthy ideas were. He could feel them, in fact, as complete empathic downloads of information. Through that process, by observing these dark areas — or "areas of limitation," as he called them — he learned he could shine his consciousness, his love, and his connection to the Divine on that particular part of the being, and he could shift it.

He said that in the week he had been with his family, he had discovered that every single thought and emotion was given to him, as he referred to it, as a direct download. He could change them because his frequency had elevated to the realm of love, and love heals everything. He was given a physical demonstration of this.

It took many conversations for me to understand this, and it took some tears and consoling on both our parts to get through those first few days. It was challenging and frightening because we did not know where this would take us. As he regained his strength, we talked more and more and resolved the confusion about the weeks that had transpired, the separation, and why it had looked the way it did. Yes, I had some forgiveness work to do with him. I had some walls up that he very kindly and gently helped me dismantle. We came to understand that a miracle had happened and that he had connected completely to another level of consciousness. In fact, he had connected to a completely different world. We would have to live and work with that enhanced, miraculous, and healing energy that was making itself known through his consciousness.

CHAPTER 27

Learning to Cope with New Energies

AS WE CONTINUED ON DAY BY DAY, WE LEARNED MORE AND MORE. We learned that Jesus's energies were powerful, and his ego mind had to be deconstructed somewhat. The practices we had been studying for so many years were key in the deconstruction processes.

We lived in a real world, just as you do, and you can imagine that if such an experience happened to you, you would have to make great adjustments. It was the same for us. We had interactions with friends and family and other routines that were disrupted by this event, and people close to us knew something extremely momentous had happened. Jesus had disappeared, and there had been a lot of concern. Everyone wanted to know what had happened. We tried to keep it cool and quiet, but like any small community, there was a great deal of interest in anything unusual.

Rumors spread, and stories were told. Some of those stories were true, and some were not. Some trickled down through the years and spawned inaccuracies about his life. We worked solidly as a couple through this entire time, and as challenging as that was, it became the most exciting time of our life, bar none! We had gone through an idyllic honeymoon phase (as you call it in your world), but at this point, we were dealing with the most magnificent manifestation of enlightenment. It was like driving a powerful new car in your world. You sometimes press the gas pedal to the floor too quickly and scare yourself a little bit. That was very much what it was like for Jesus.

He worked to manage the energy, negotiating how it functioned in his body and examining how it made him feel. At times he was very confused about what this meant. No instruction booklet came with this enlightenment, and he knew he would have to figure it out for himself. He continued to receive direct communications from Spirit just as he had his entire life, but his new teachers did not live in physical bodies in homes with children and wives, and he had to learn to negotiate many new things (not the least of which was the fact that he didn't need to eat as much food).

The next few months were spent learning how to handle the energy as well as other people. This was not an easy journey for those close to him, either. His students and his fellow teachers were all different, and they had a variety of reactions. Some left the community of study in which we had been immersed for so many years because they did not know what was happening, and their ideas of possession and demons were triggered. Great fears arose in them. Other beings were so awed by him that they weren't able to function in his presence. Then there were a number of reactions in between those extremes. We negotiated relationships with other people, and after several months, we decided it was time for Jesus to begin a teaching practice that employed the new energies. He had been surreptitiously healing people because he could see their afflictions or what was upsetting them when he talked to them. People began to feel much better in his presence.

People began to feel extreme peace because their minds were calmed by the frequency that he exuded, and he exuded it passively. People could feel his presence and the light and love coming from him. But if he focused his mind and directed that strength of energy and compassion at somebody, he could remove whatever caused that person's trouble. He learned that this was not always an easy thing for people to handle. When someone had been sick for a long time and organizing life around that illness and developing relationships based on it, healing it often created a real shake up not only in the mental structure of the person who had been ill but also in the people around him or her. Many would question their world or what they considered their reality.

The healing Jesus shared began to disrupt people's peace of minds, and he saw that he needed to teach them about love and the shifts in frequency that he had gone through. However, they had no language with which to understand the profound spiritual growth and acceleration he had experienced. Remember, he had been a very studious practitioner who was well educated and well read, and this was not the case for most people. They were ordinary beings living ordinary lives. So he had to put the teachings into words those people could understand, and that is, of course, how his parables came about.

Gathering the Disciples

It was decided that he would once again take his ministry on the road, and this time, he intentionally gathered the group of beings you know as his Disciples. They came to him through various meetings in a relatively short period. Clearly, these beings were directed to him just as he was directed to gather a group of supporters. Some of this was for protection. In some ways, they were his bodyguards. "Entourage" is the modern word you use for it. There were various personalities and levels of spiritual development in the group, and some of the beings were even related to him. He had a very good support system when he was away from home.

That was the beginning of the ministry you have heard about, but it was not exactly as you have heard. He was very conscientious about bringing women into the picture, whom he taught specifically and privately. These were wives and daughters and sisters of the men in the audiences who were open to hearing about equality and the sacredness of all beings and all life and the removal of judgment. Of course, this is what antiwoman philosophies employ: negative judgments about the value of women. Jesus directly dealt with that issue.

This too caused a great deal of confusion. People lived in a strictly patriarchal society, and women were not seen as equals, so these were revolutionary teachings.

He and I talked about these things when he came home from his journeys, and it became clear that the arrangement we had of my staying at home, looking after the children, and keeping everything calm and happy worked well for him. He would come home after days of teaching and preaching and healing, and he would be very tired and sometimes overwhelmed by the assignment he had been given. You must understand that he did not pick this consciously from his separated ego consciousness. It seemed to happen to him, and it caused a lot of handwringing and head holding on his part. We sat together in silence on many nights praying for guidance, understanding, and clarity on where this path would lead us. Early on, he was told that this ministry would not last long and that he would be required to leave the Earth plane before he was an old man and had satisfied my desire for a long marriage.

This caused a great deal of upset on my part. I had young children, and I loved this man more than life itself. The thought of losing him terrified me. He was patient, and as distressing as it was for both of us to hear this information, he was assured through communications from Spirit that all would be arranged so that no suffering on my part or his part would transpire despite the challenges we faced in this new experience. We did not suffer because we had been taught many techniques to shift the consciousness into one of peace and love, and we continued to do that when we felt fear or any kind of suffering. One of us was always saner than the other, so we worked together, and Jesus made no bones about the fact that it was his quiet and peaceful home life, focused on prayer and meditation and peace, that helped him through the challenging and busy times of being on the road, teaching and preaching.

CHAPTER 28

Transcending the Physical World

JESUS WORKED AS A HEALER AND A TEACHER AND TRAVELED TO VARIOUS towns every other week or so to do intensive, on-the-ground teaching. His channeled information from nonphysical beings was very intense at that time, as he was literally fed information the week before he was to teach it and then debriefed after each experience. It was very hard on him to be around so many people, to be swarmed and intimidated; that was the most difficult part for him. That was why I did not go with him. I provided support by staying home so that he could have a place to return to and recover from his excursions.

The number of people who wanted him and the number of hours he put in on those journeys were tremendous. He slept and ate little. When he spent time with me, he used it for recuperation because he was exhausted after seven or ten days of ministering. Traveling was tiring in those days. There were no fast, comfortable, air-conditioned cars; instead, there was a lot of walking physical exertion. Violence erupted around his teaching. The Romans were intimidated when they realized he brought joy and hope to the minds and hearts of those he spoke with, and the Jewish hierarchies were very upset. They had a stranglehold on the population, and Jesus pried their fingers off the people's throats as they struggled for air. He was that breath of fresh air, a bringer of truth and love and optimism for those who felt oppressed by the many levels of government.

He was warned and attacked time and again by various groups of be-ings who did not want him to do what he did, which is why he had twelve disciples to care for and provide for him. They were a somewhat intim-idating group who could protect him. That is not covered in your Bible, but it was very much a part of the rationale of having that many men around him. It kept him safe and brought him home to me.

At that time, our relationship was deeply challenged by the teach-ings. We had young children, and he missed them terribly, but his guid-ance from the nonphysical showed him the way. We talked about the fact that his time on Earth was limited, which was not an easy thing for me. During the two years or so that we knew this would transpire, we worked through the emotions. His teachers spoke through him to me, much as this being's teachers speaks through her to you, and they explained that his time on Earth was necessarily short, that it was the arrangement. They said we would understand what was going on as we traveled through our incarnation. They said he had been designated as a bringer of light to do this, but it was not a long-term shift, so to speak; it was a short shift.

I was told that I would be cared for and that the transformation and transfiguration he would go through would seem to be very difficult, but the life I would lead as a result of this experience would be perfectly hap-py. It was difficult for me to understand this, and it was very, very hard for Jesus to accept it as well, despite his enlightenment.

He loved me and our children, and he loved his life as it was, but as time passed, it became clear that he was drastically changing from an ordinary physical human being into something else. He was much less concerned with worldly things and spent more and more time in medi-tation and communing with these higher realms, and I could see that he was no longer attached to the world in the way that ordinary conscious-ness is. He was no longer attached to the body in the way that ordinary consciousness is, and he began to experiment with transforming it. He experimented with leaving his body for long periods. I would find him meditating, and he would be gone for hours. He was simply not there. So these were some of the preparations that took place to and through him as we approached that time you call the Crucifixion.

Fulfilling the Agreement

This is where the story really diverts from your understanding of events. He went to the crucifixion completely knowledgeable and intentionally teaching. He spent a lot of time with the children and me in those last few months. That is not documented in your mythology, but that is what happened. As the date approached, he knew it was coming. It was his decision, not something that was forced on him. There were circumstances set up by Spirit to make it appear that it happened to him, but he knew — and he had known since his enlightenment — that this was going to transpire.

Part of his teaching was to show that the body is not of value; it is "repeatable," if you will, for it can be made anew. He taught that the physical realm is a low realm and there were many others above it. This gave people an incentive to study and practice his teachings so that they could learn that they were heading toward a wonderful, wonderful experience.

As he went to his crucifixion fully knowledgeable, aware, and accepting of what would happen, he knew he would not suffer. He knew he could remove his consciousness from his body and that the play that looked very vicious, violent, and murderous was merely that: It was a play, and he was not in it. He was above it.

The day of his crucifixion was, however, one of the worst days of my life because I saw somebody I loved go through what looked like devastating torture. I was with Jesus on the walk and at the crucifixion, and as I looked into his eyes, I could see he knew and that he was fine. He was there and not there. He was okay. But it was impossible for me to remain calm. My ordinary consciousness (remember, I wasn't enlightened at this point) could not tolerate what his captors did to him. As the day passed, it was clear he had left his physical structure; it was merely surviving on what you call a lower level of consciousness, a vegetative state. It functioned just as your structure does when you are asleep: It breathes and digests (that too was happening to him at the end), among other functions. But he had gone. The higher levels of his consciousness had moved on, and I was prepared for the next stage of the game, so to speak.

He had told me that we would meet again shortly after this experience and that I was to be the first to see him. This is where you can go to your Bible and get some sense that I was significant in his life, but your Bible does not offer anything truthful, really, about his ministry, because it had an agenda. The people who wrote it had an agenda, and they wanted to make him something that he was not.

He was a being who studied frequency elevation and spiritual practices that were given to him by nonphysical teachers. He studied with physical teachers and incorporated those practices into his. He unceasingly aligned himself with love, and in that alignment, he overcame the separated, physical world, the material world. That is all he ever wanted to teach people: that they could do it too and that is the truth. You all can do it.

As we put his killed and empty body to rest, I felt a sense of peace. I knew it was part of the teaching. However, this did not go very well with many of the Disciples. They were not privy to the same intimate conversations and preparations I'd had with Jesus, so they went into fear and terror. However, a couple of them knew, through their close association with Jesus and me, what was happening and why, and they were able to handle a very challenging time.

This is difficult for you to comprehend because of your indoctrinations, but the journey that I went on with Jesus through his ministry, crucifixion, resurrection, and the rest of my life were joyful despite the intensity of that week. It was amazing to see an enlightened person go through the ultimate experiment, if you will, of being killed and having the mastery of the physical/material world to return completely healthy in a new physical form. That is exactly what happened. We reunited at the designated time, and he was himself. This became the private part of our relationship. It is not written about in your books, in your mythology, yet after that event, we continued on for many, many years as husband and wife.

You must revise your opinion of me and of Jesus to come to an understanding of what you are. We were no different from you. We had our assignments in our incarnations, and you have your assignments in yours. Your incarnational assignments are hidden in your feeling self, in your desires, your passions, and the truth of the peace of your mind. When your mind is at peace and you are in that inner guidance, then you are on the true path to enlightenment. There is no secret here. God has not hidden the answer in some cryptic, sacrificial practice. It is in love that you find your way Home. It is in love that you express your true nature and reach this place of awakening and eternal life. There is no death as you know it; that is an illusory concept that becomes true when you believe in it. Because Jesus did not believe in it anymore, he overcame death. He went through a public demonstration of something that was not survivable, yet his consciousness created a new body.

This was the miracle he wanted to teach to his Disciples, but because they had absolute love and adoration for him without the intimate knowledge I had of him, they could not tolerate the experience and the teaching. It became distorted, and many of them reverted to their conditioned ways. Remember, they had not had long relationships with him; some of them had only known him for three years. So they were not able to complete their transformation of mind. I completed my transformation of mind during our marriage and those years of the ministry, and I was prepared. I knew what he could do. He had shown me what he could do, and even though it was a traumatic thing to witness, it was not the truth of my understanding, so I did not experience it the way you would imagine. As difficult as it was, it was not the end that other people thought it was.

CHAPTER 29

The Magnificent Journey through God's Heart

AS YOU CAN IMAGINE, SUCCEEDING IN THAT PARTICULAR EPIC JOURNEY and coming out the other side was the culmination of several years of physical, emotional, and mental preparation. It was a difficult journey, and I went through hell (in some ways) as I watched that body be brutalized and crucified and killed. It was a demonstration of mastery that was unbelievable to many, and that was the most difficult thing for Jesus. The psychological effects of witnessing that death and then the miracle of the reconstruction of a new body were too much for many of the Disciples.

They were relatively new in spiritual practice. Despite their time with Jesus, they were young men who had a hard time shifting in consciousness. They had not gone through the decades of practice that several of us had, so they reverted to the mind in which they were more comfortable, which was the traditional Jewish teachings. It brought up for them terrors of demons and possession, much as it would for you in your society. You too have been indoctrinated in beliefs of demons and evil, and this is a great detriment to your frequency.

We ask you to look at that aspect of yourself. Do you believe in demons? Do you believe in their ability to affect you or "get you" or come randomly into your experience? These are beliefs that must be cleansed from the mind through prayer and by focusing on love and higher consciousness so that these unloving and unhealthy beliefs do not sabotage you. Because of such fears, the Disciples who chose to leave after the res-urrection lost a great opportunity to continue studying with the master, with my beloved Jesus.

After the resurrection, Jesus and I remained in our home area for sever-al weeks, but because of what had transpired, it became impossible for us to stay there. We had children and families, and it was time to end that chapter of our lives. We could not stay in a place where many had witnessed his death. We could not stay with people who grieved his death even though he was alive and well. They were not able to process the information, and it became clear that there would be a big shift in our life together. In quiet contemplation and conversation, we decided to leave our home. We took our children, yes, and we moved to a different part of the world. Of course, we didn't view it that way then, but we knew we would go on a journey across the water to another land. That is what we decided to do. If the Dis-ciples could not handle the truth of Jesus's resurrection, then surely neither could ordinary people. So we decided as a team, as an equal couple, that our public work was done, our public life was over, and we would live out our lives in the way we wanted to, which was in quiet contemplation in a rural, gentle, and less troubled place.

Together, we recruited the two Disciples who had been able to work with and manage the energies and transformation that Jesus had gone through, and we sailed to the region you call the South of France, where we sought out a place to live. It was a different life for me. It was a diffi-cult time, but I was with the beings I loved with all my heart and soul. It was hard to leave my home, but it had changed. It was not a place where I could reside in peace, and it was not a place where I wanted to raise my children. I wanted to raise my children in a peaceful, calm, and loving environment that would benefit them. I did not feel that the fractious and oppressive — and at times combative and aggressive — place would be the best, so I made the difficult decision to leave one part of my life and begin another.

You must understand that we made that journey together. I was not abandoned in any way, shape, or form, so I was not afraid. I knew I had a powerful spiritual teacher as my partner. I had a powerful spiritual teach-er as my guide, as my husband, and as the father of my children, so I was in safekeeping. Spirit had said I would not have to suffer very long, and in fact, the suffering I experienced in my life was very short-lived. The suffering I experienced was only during the crucifixion and the subsequent times of separation, which came from within my own mind. Those challenges taught me something about how to discipline my mind and how to focus on what I wanted, the outcome I wanted more of.

We took our very challenging life lessons and moved to a place where we could live in peace and harmony as a relatively anonymous couple. Jesus, of course, was not the kind of person who disappeared in a crowd. He made himself known in that environment and began to teach once again, but he was changed. He had gone through a massive shift in consciousness, as his enlightenment required, and after the resurrection, there was another shift in him that was irrevocable. It was not negative, but I guess it caused me to lose some connection with him. He needed to be with Spirit more and more.

He needed to separate from the physical world more and more. He no longer needed it. It was meaningless to him. The games, the words, and the choices that people made were not his, and he did not really identify with them anymore. Even his connection with his children was affected. It was not that he did not love or care about them, but he was no longer bound by the physical/material world, and he spent a lot of time in other places in meditation. He would meditate for days at a time and then would return into his body and consciousness to participate in life.

He journeyed far and wide in those years, and as we matured and came into our middle years (of course, he did not age; he was not subject to the laws of physics as I still was at that time), we became more like brother and sister. This is not something for those of you who are romantics to be sad about. Do not see this as the ultimate testimony to the unfairness of the world; that is not so. We loved each other purely in spirit. We had experienced our passionate younger years, had our children, and endured the tumult and the disruption of his public ministry. We were happy to live the way we were living.

I had not had a normal life, and we had not had an ordinary life together. We hadn't asked for normal. And we want you to not ask for normal, either. You have been taught to live limited lives just as I was when I was a young woman. I was taught to be subservient, and I was taught that women were not valued as highly as men. I grew beyond that with my beloved teaching me and helping to heal my mind and bring it into balance. Honoring myself as well as him was a most magnificent journey. But I had to be prepared to be abnormal and not look like everybody else, and I was willing to do that to have the experience that I had.

I was in the place you call the South of France for a long time — from my early thirties until I passed into the nonphysical, and during that time, Jesus taught in that area. I taught there too, and there were followers, beings who listened and took these teachings to heart. There is a culture, based on those teachings, that grew up in that area, and it is a valid organization and interpretation, albeit not particularly accurate on what transpired.

The teachings came to that part of the world and spread over the centuries to other areas. They were not accepted. They were always considered rebellious because they do not support the hierarchical structures of the organized church, and they never have and never will. They are freedom-seeking, love-based teachings, and they ask you to listen to your inner guidance as the authority you follow from birth to death. If you do, if you practice what we teach through these texts and *A Course in Miracles*, you will, in the end, avoid the death you fear so much. It is an illusory concept that is only active in your life if you believe in it.

Add Love to Everything

As you mature, evolve, and grow, relinquishing judgment, separation, and fear, and choosing love day after day, hour after hour, and moment after moment, you will align with frequencies that do not require you to die in the way you believe you have to. It is a time-consuming activity, and it requires dedication and practice, but we want you to know that the life you lead without these ideas and thoughts of forgiveness and love is not worth living. You live in separation and the fear of death and poverty, and in fact, you bring these things to you because you believe in them. As you believe more and more in Spirit, in the Divine, and in love and you practice it not only in your actions and your words but in your thoughts and in your feelings, you will manifest things in your world that you could not manifest before.

This is the path to peace and happiness, and as I came to the end of my life, Jesus met me and took me into his arms, and we walked together into that nonphysical world that you call the afterlife. It is not after life; it is life, life, life, life. You never die. You are an eternal spiritual being, and you are completely in alignment with love all the time. Any suffering you experience is your mind dipping into fear or shame or jealousy or anger or scarcity, and it is not the reality of who you are.

Love is real. Love is the answer to all the problems on your planet at this time. It is the answer to all the problems you have in your world, your life, your body, and your relationships. Add love to everything. It is how Jesus and I got through that most magnificent incarnation together. I have no regrets. I experienced something that very few people have experienced, but as your planet evolves and more and more of you align with love, more of you will have these kinds of experiences.

We want you know that you have the ability to align with love, and that is all Jesus and I did. We aligned ourselves with love, and we reaped the rewards of that most magnificent crop. You always reap what you sow, so pay attention to your thoughts, your feelings, and these lessons. They are impeccable and invaluable, and they will take you on a journey into the heart of God; nothing else will do for you.

I am the one you know as Mary Magdalene, and I will share teachings in the next few years with my beloved Jesus. These are important times, and you must focus your hearts and minds on what you want and what makes you happy, and that is love. It is always love.

About the Author

TINA LOUISE SPALDING WAS RAISED IN A FAMILY that often visited psychics, so she is no stranger to the nonphysical world. Her channeling journey began when she settled down for a nap on the summer solstice of 2012. That afternoon, powerful energies began to surge through her body, leading to ecstasy, bliss, and an altered state of consciousness that lasted for almost a month. The feelings finally drove her to take an automatic writing workshop, where she was first made aware of Ananda. She then began to write for this group of nonphysical teachers who have come to assist us in our waking process.

Tina began channeling Jesus in the summer of 2013, when he appeared in her book *Great Minds Speak to You*. It proved to be a great challenge not only to accept the assignment he offered her — writing his autobiography — but also face many of the fears that this unusual experience brought up. Tina has been asked to channel for Jesus on an ongoing basis. Check her website, ChannelingJesus.com, for public offerings of his teachings.

Tina speaks for Ananda as a full trance channel, offering teachings and personal readings for those who seek more happiness, fulfillment, and connection with Spirit. She has dedicated her life to writing and speaking for Ananda and other nonphysical beings, sharing their wisdom and spiritual knowledge.

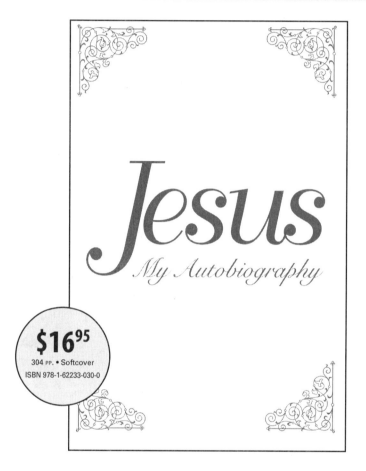

BY TINA LOUISE SPALDING

GREAT MINDS SPEAK TO YOU

With CD

"Many in spirit look on these times of difficulty, abundance, trouble, and innovation and wish to share with you their experiences and ideas. Some famous names and faces will come to mind as you read this book, and you will glean some fine information about their learning, their suffering, and indeed their experience in the life after this life, for they all wish to tell you that there is no death as you perceive it to be. They are all there in their astral forms, enjoying their continued growth, their continued expansion, and their continued joy in living.

"Their messages are as varied as their lives were, and our purpose is this: For you to understand your true nature, your true potential, you must let go of your fear of death, for it makes you afraid to live. It causes you to rush and panic, to become scared, and to become paralyzed. When you truly understand that you are eternal beings, forgiven for all your errors and blamed for nothing that you would call a sin, you will open your hearts and minds to so much more and enjoy yourselves so much more. You would not suffer so at the loss of your loved ones, and you would work less and achieve more, for when you are in fear and grief, you are not yourselves and cannot achieve the goals that have set for yourselves before you decided to be born onto this plane you call life.

"Read this with an open mind and heart, and hear what these beings have to say. You have revered and reviled them in life; now let them complete their stories in what you call death, for that is the complete story. Is it not?"

— Ananda

$19⁹⁵ Softcover, 192 PP.
ISBN 978-1-62233-010-2

CHAPTERS INCLUDE
- Albert Einstein
- Jerry Garcia
- Ralph Waldo Emerson
- Marilyn Monroe
- John Huston
- Amy Winehouse
- Margaret Thatcher
- Princess Diana
- Susan B. Anthony
- Sylvia Plath
- Elizabeth Taylor
- John and Robert Kennedy
- Michael Jackson
- Cecil B. DeMille
- Jonas Salk
- Queen Mother Elizabeth
- George Bernard Shaw
- Pablo Picasso
- John Lennon

☙ Light Technology PUBLISHING Presents

BY TOM T. MOORE

THE GENTLE WAY
A SELF-HELP GUIDE FOR THOSE WHO BELIEVE IN ANGELS

"This book is for people of all faiths and beliefs with the only requirement being a basic belief in angels. It will put you back in touch with your guardian angel or strengthen and expand the connection that you may already have. How can I promise these benefits? Because I have been using these concepts for over ten years and I can report these successes from direct knowledge and experience. But this is a self-help guide, so that means it requires your active participation." — Tom T. Moore

$14.⁹⁵ • 160 PP., SOFTCOVER • ISBN 978-1-891824-60-9

THE GENTLE WAY II
BENEVOLENT OUTCOMES: THE STORY CONTINUES

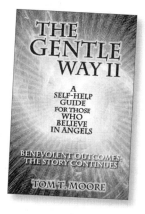

You'll be amazed at how easy it is to be in touch with guardian angels and how much assistance you can receive simply by asking. This inspirational self-help book, written for all faiths and beliefs, explains how there is a more benevolent world that we can access, and how we can achieve this.

This unique and incredibly simple technique assists you in manifesting your goals easily and effortlessly for the first time. It works quickly, sometimes with immediate results, and no affirmations, written intentions, or changes in behavior are needed. You don't even have to believe in it for it to work!

$16.⁹⁵ • 320 PP., SOFTCOVER • ISBN 978-1-891824-80-7

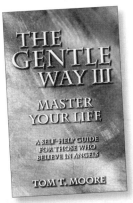

THE GENTLE WAY III
MASTER YOUR LIFE

"Almost three years have passed since *The Gentle Way II* was published. Yet as many success stories as that book contained, I have continued to receive truly unique stories from people all over the world requesting most benevolent outcomes and asking for benevolent prayers for their families, friends, other people, and other beings. It just proves that there are no limits to this modality, which is becoming a gentle movement as people discover how much better their lives are with these simple yet powerful requests." — Tom T. Moore

$16.⁹⁵ • 352 PP., SOFTCOVER • ISBN 978-1-62233-005-8

☥ *Light Technology* PUBLISHING *Presents*

THROUGH RAE CHANDRAN

32 color pages of mudras and images to activate your 12 levels of DNA

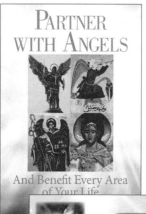

DNA of the Spirit, Volume 1

The etheric strands of your DNA are the information library of your soul. They contain the complete history of you, lifetime after lifetime; a record of the attitudes, karma, and emotional predispositions you brought into this lifetime; and a blueprint, or lesson plan, for your self-improvement.
$19.95 • Softcover • 384 PP.
ISBN 978-1-62233-013-3

DNA of the Spirit, Volume 2

This companion book to *DNA of the Spirit, Volume 1* originated with the intention and desire to bring forth understanding to support humanity. Go through this volume while holding a sacredness inside of you, asking that the material be imprinted in your sacredness so that it may become an experience that you will be able to live.
$16.95 • Softcover • 192 PP.
ISBN 978-1-62233-027-0

Dance of the Hands

Dance of the Hands is for everyone, not just people who are spiritually advanced. It is for any layperson, regardless of religion. This material is for those who have an interest in bet-

tering themselves or improving their well-being — practitioners, teachers, masters, the spiritually advanced, neophytes, and children.
$16.95 • Softcover • 160 PP.
Wire-O bound
ISBN 978-1-62233-038-6

Partner with Angels

Angels are the Creator's workforce, and in this book, individual angels describe their responsibilities and explain how they can help you with all aspects of your life — practical and spiritual. All you need to do is ask.
$16.95 • Softcover • 208 PP.
ISBN 978-1-62233-034-8

Angels and Ascension

Angels are available with all kinds of help. This must become part of your reality. Set your antenna to the angels, and communicate with them. All of life's miracles happen with angelic presence. When you begin to do this, you will see that you have an ever-present friend at your shoulder.
$16.95 • Softcover • 128 PP.
ISBN 978-1-62233-048-5

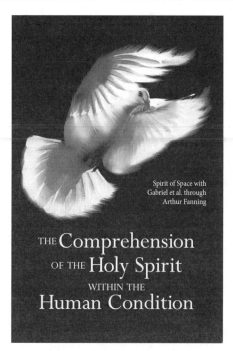
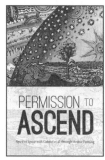

THROUGH ROBERT SHAPIRO

Shamanic Secrets Series

Speaks of Many Truths, Zoosh, and Reveals the Mysteries through Robert Shapiro

Shamanic Secrets for Material Mastery

This book explores the heart and soul connection between humans and Earth. Through that intimacy, miracles of healing and expanded awareness can flourish. To heal the planet and be healed as well, you can lovingly extend your energy self out to the mountains and rivers and intimately bond with Earth. Gestures and vision can activate your heart to return you to a healthy, caring relationship with the land you live on. The character of some of Earth's most powerful features is explored and understood with exercises given to connect you with those places. As you project your love and healing energy there, you help Earth to heal from human destruction of the planet and its atmosphere. Dozens of photographs, maps, and drawings assist the process in twenty-five chapters, which cover Earth's more critical locations.

SOFTCOVER • 512 PP. • $19.95 • ISBN 978-1-891824-12-8

Shamanic Secrets for Physical Mastery

Learn to understand the sacred nature of your physical body and some of the magnificent gifts it offers you. When you work with your physical body in these new ways, you will discover not only its sacredness but also how it is compatible with Mother Earth, the animals, the plants, and even the nearby planets, all of which you now recognize as being sacred in nature. It is important to feel the value of oneself physically before you can have any lasting physical impact on the world. If a physical energy does not feel good about itself, it will usually be resolved; other physical or spiritual energies will dissolve it because they are unnatural. The better you feel about your physical self when you do the work in the first book, as well as this one and the one to follow, the greater and more lasting the benevolent effect will be on your life, on the lives of those around you, and ultimately on your planet and universe.

SOFTCOVER • 576 PP. • $25.00 • ISBN 978-1-891824-29-6

Shamanic Secrets for Spiritual Mastery

"Spiritual mastery encompasses many different means to assimilate and be assimilated by the wisdom, feelings, flow, warmth, function, and application of all beings in your world that you will actually contact in some way. A lot of spiritual mastery has been covered in different bits and pieces throughout all the books we've done. My approach to spiritual mastery, though, will be as grounded as possible in things that people on Earth can use — but it won't include the broad spectrum of spiritual mastery, like levitation and invisibility. My life is basically going to represent your needs, and in a storylike fashion it gets out the secrets that have been held back."

— Speaks of Many Truths

SOFTCOVER • 768 PP. • $29.95 • ISBN 978-1-891824-58-6

THROUGH ROBERT SHAPIRO

Are You a Walk-In?

"This book is intended to be practical advice for day-to-day living for people who know they are walk-ins, for people who believe they might be walk-ins, for the family and friends and business associates of people who are believed to be walk-ins or may believe they are walk-ins themselves. In short, this book is intended to serve the community to understand the walk-in phenomenon and for those who are experiencing it personally, to be able to apply it in such a way as they are able to live easier, more comfortable, more useful, and more fulfilling lives."

— Reveals the Mystery through Robert Shapiro

$19.95 • Softcover • 304 PP. • ISBN 978-1-891824-40-1

ARE YOU A WALK-IN?

A NEW FORM OF BENEVOLENT BIRTH
IS NOW AVAILABLE ON EARTH

Zoosh, Isis, Reveals the Mysteries, and More
through **Robert Shapiro**

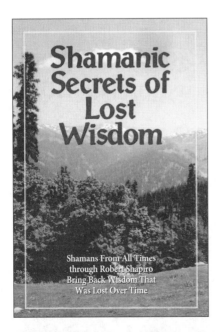

Shamanic Secrets of Lost Wisdom

Shamans From All Times
through Robert Shapiro
Bring Back Wisdom That
Was Lost Over Time

Shamanic Secrets of Lost Wisdom

Ninety-five percent of shamanic wisdom gained over the course of time on Earth has been lost. Now, through ancient shamans in spirit speaking through channel Robert Shapiro, this wisdom has been found. It is available for present humans to use to heal, survive, and increase the quality of their lives.

$19.95 • Softcover • 356 PP. • ISBN 978-1-62233-049-2

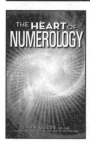

☼ *Light Technology* PUBLISHING *Presents*

TO ORDER PRINT BOOKS
Visit LightTechnology.com, Call 928-526-1345 or 1-800-450-0985,
or Check Amazon.com or Your Favorite Bookstore

BOOKS THROUGH JAAP VAN ETTEN

Birth of a New Consciousness: Dialogues with the Sidhe

This book contains the wisdom of the Sidhe, a race of human-like beings who are our direct relatives. They are invisible to our five senses and occupy one of the subtle worlds that are part of Gaia.

Embark on a journey, the journey of every soul who comes to Earth. This book stimulates you to raise your vibration and expand your view of reality by giving many suggestions on how to do so. It truly can be called the start of a new consciousness.

$16.95 • Softcover • 6 x 9 • 192 PP. • ISBN 978-1-62233-033-1

CRYSTAL SKULLS: Expand Your Consciousness

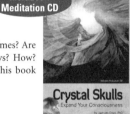

Includes 1 Meditation CD

Crystal skulls invoke a sense of mystery. What was their role in ancient times? Are they important for us now? Can they assist us on our spiritual journeys? How? Although much has been written about them, many questions linger. This book addresses these questions on practical, subtle-energy, and spiritual levels.

$25.00 • 256 PP. • Softcover • ISBN 978-1-62233-000-3

CRYSTAL SKULLS: Interacting with a Phenomenon

Discover your energetic connection with crystal skulls. Learn how to utilize these energies for your own personal growth and how these special energies affect your awareness and expand your consciousness.

$19.95 • 240 PP. • Softcover • ISBN 978-1-891824-64-7

Gifts of Mother Earth

We live in a sea of energies that are part of the Earth we live on. Most people are not aware of these energies and consequently are not aware that they hold many gifts. These gifts help us to heal, balance, expand consciousness (awareness), and support spiritual evolution. Our ancestors knew the gifts of Mother Earth and used these energies to support their lives and spirituality in many ways. We, modern humans, have mostly forgotten that they exist.

$16.95 • 256 PP. • Softcover • ISBN 978-1-891824-86-9

☿ *Light Technology* PUBLISHING *Presents*

TO ORDER PRINT BOOKS
Visit LightTechnology.com, Call 928-526-1345 or 1-800-450-0985,
or Check Amazon.com or Your Favorite Bookstore

THROUGH DAVID K. MILLER

Fifth-Dimensional Soul Psychology

"The basic essence of soul psychology rests with the idea that the soul is evolving and that part of this evolution is occurring through incarnations in the third dimension. Now, to even speak about the soul evolving is perhaps a controversial subject because we know that the soul is eternal. We know that the soul has been in existence for infinity, and we know that the soul is perfect. So why would the soul have to evolve?

The answer to this question is complex, and we may not be able to totally answer it using third-dimensional terminology. But it is an important question to answer because the nature of soul evolution is inherently connected to your experiences in the third dimension. The soul, in completing its evolutionary journey, needs these experiences in the third dimension, and it needs to complete the lessons here."

—Vywamus

$16.95 • 288 PP. • Softcover • 978-1-62233-016-4

Teachings from the Sacred Triangle, Volume 1

The first book of the Sacred Triangle series explains how the Arcturian energy melds with that of the White Brother-Sisterhood and the ascended Native American masters to bring about planetary healing.

Topics include the Sacred Triangle energy and the sacred codes of ascension, how to create a bridge to the fifth dimension, what role you can play in the Sacred Triangle, and how sacred words from the Kaballah can assist you in your ascension work.

$16.95 • 272 PP. • Softcover • 978-1-62233-007-2

Teachings from the Sacred Triangle, Volume 2

Our planet is at a dire crossroads from a physical standpoint, but from a spiritual standpoint, it is experiencing a great awakening. Never before have there been so many conscious lightworkers, awakened spiritual beings, and masters as there are on this planet now. A great sense of a spiritual harmony emanates from the many starseed groups, and there is also a new spiritual energy and force that is spreading throughout the planet.

$16.95 • 288 PP. • Softcover • 978-1-891824-19-7

Teachings from the Sacred Triangle, Volume 3

Learn how to use holographic technology to project energies in the most direct and transformative way throughout Earth. It will not be necessary to travel to distant places. When you interact with the part of Earth you are familiar with, you can affect the entire planet. Any part of the whole that has been distorted can be transformed into a fifth-dimensional holographic energy.

$16.95 • 288 PP. • Softcover • 978-1-891824-23-4

Expand Your Consciousness

Now more than ever, humankind is in need of developing its higher consciousness to heal itself and Earth and to experience life in a much more meaningful way. By expanding in consciousness, we can see the connections and unity that exist in all reality, and we might see objects with sharper colors, hear sounds with greater clarity, or even experience two sensations simultaneously! In this book, you will explore the fascinating multidimensionality that is yours for the taking.

$16.95 • 288 PP. • Softcover • 978-1-62233-036-2

Enseñanzas del Sagrado Triángulo Arcturiano

Este paradigma es necesario para ayudar en la transición de la humanidad hacia la próxima etapa evolutiva. La humanidad debe realizar esta próxima etapa de la evolución, para asegurar su sobrevivencia por los cambios climáticos globales, la guerra y la destrucción del medio ambiente. ¿Cuál es la próxima etapa? Esta involucra la expansión de la consciencia del ser humano y está representada por el símbolo de este nuevo paradigma, el Sagrado Triángulo Arcturiano.

El guía de la quinta dimensión, Juliano, proveniente del sistema estelar galáctico conocido como Arcturus, trabaja junto a David en un papel prominente en esta introducción de la energía del Triángulo Sagrado en la Tierra. David le ofrece al lector un entendimiento del alma, su naturaleza evolutiva y como la humanidad esta avanzando hacia esa siguiente etapa evolutiva.

$19.95 • 416 PP. • Softcover • 978-1-62233-264-9